T0316817

WHY THE WORLD ECONOMY NEEDS A FINANCIAL CRASH AND OTHER CRITICAL ESSAYS ON FINANCE AND FINANCIAL ECONOMICS

Advance Praise

'Jan Toporowski is the best-kept secret in British economics. His insightful essays combine insight into current market mechanisms and macroeconomic dynamics with a keen appreciation of the historical sources of the ideas being debated in today's financial pages. This book explains Toporowski's ground-breaking theory of financial inflation, which is the key to understanding why financial-market forces ultimately exploded. In sum, this book answers questions readers didn't know they had about the 2007–08 financial crisis and about all the financial crises in the neoliberal era.'
—*Gary Dymski, Professor of Economics, University of California, Riverside*

'Jan Toporowski offers a lively and engaging critical assessment of national and international financial problems. He writes clearly, in non-technical language, and explores the economic, historical, political, cultural and symbolic significance of finance. Anyone with a serious interest in the "great recession" that began in 2007 will benefit from reading this book.'
—*John King, Professor of Economics, La Trobe University*

'In these essays Jan Toporowski demonstrates his characteristic ability to combine analytical insights with policy relevant commentary on a range of topics associated with financial inflation and with baking and financial crises. Directed at a non-technical audience, the discussions offer a lesson in rigor, clarity and conciseness. The breath of knowledge is impressive and the resulting analyses always telling and thought-provoking. A book to be highly recommended.'
—*Grahame F. Thompson, Professor of Political Economy, The Open University and Visiting Professor at the Copenhagen Business School*

'Offers a uniquely systemic and historically aware insight into the structural, institutional, socio-political and cultural origins of financial instability associated with the rise of global finance... A sharp and comprehensive critique of the financial orthodoxy that is behind many myths of contemporary economics and political economy.'
—*Anastasia Nesvetailova, Department of International Politics, School of Social Sciences, City University London*

WHY THE WORLD ECONOMY NEEDS A FINANCIAL CRASH

AND OTHER CRITICAL ESSAYS ON FINANCE AND FINANCIAL ECONOMICS

JAN TOPOROWSKI

ANTHEM PRESS
LONDON · NEW YORK · DELHI

Anthem Press
An imprint of Wimbledon Publishing Company
www.anthempress.com

This edition first published in UK and USA 2010
by ANTHEM PRESS
75-76 Blackfriars Road, London SE1 8HA, UK
or PO Box 9779, London SW19 7ZG, UK
and
244 Madison Ave. #116, New York, NY 10016, USA

British Library Cataloguing in Publication Data
A catalogue record for this book is available from the British Library.

Library of Congress Cataloging in Publication Data
Toporowski, Jan.
Why the world economy needs a financial crash and other critical
essays on finance and financial economics / Jan Toporowski.
p. cm.
Includes bibliographical references and index.
ISBN 978-0-85728-959-9 (hardcover : alk. paper)
ISBN 978-0-85728-980-3 (papercover : alk. paper)
1. Inflation (Finance) 2. Financial crises. 3. Capital assets
pricing model. 4. Capital market. 5. International finance.
6. Business cycles. I. Title.
HG229.T67 2010
332--dc22
2010045758

ISBN-13: 978 0 85728 959 9 (Hbk)
ISBN-10: 0 85728 959 4 (Hbk)

ISBN-13: 978 0 85728 980 3 (Pbk)
ISBN-10: 0 85728 980 2 (Pbk)

This title is also available as an eBook.

Contents

Introduction

On the 19 February 1986 the *Financial Times* published my article 'Why the World Economy Needs a Financial Crash'. That article had a devastating effect on my career, leading to my virtual blacklisting in the financial institutions of the City of London. The loss of my job imposed new stresses and insecurities on my young family. It also changed the course of my intellectual development and transformed my outlook on the discussions of policy and theory that are supposed to be the vehicle for the progress of reason in economics and politics. The article was written in the belief that, in contrast to the engaged writer in an authoritarian regime, we live in an intellectual democracy in which ideas and analysis are evaluated on their merits. Publication of my article marked the turning point to my realisation that the market-place for ideas is the playground of coteries vying for or exercising power. In that playground, a special place is reserved for the media whose function is 'as an opinion board telling individual agents in the market what average or conventional opinion is at any one time'.[1] (Josef Steindl went even further and suggested that the particular coteries, or 'opinion-leaders' dominate that playground, forming the expectations of participants in financial markets to maintain a certain speculative enthusiasm or deflationary temper in those markets.[2] Arguably financial economics functions in much the same way.)

My article was written amidst the devastation caused by the Third World Debt crisis of 1982. The abandonment of the Bretton Woods system of fixed exchange rates, closely followed by the quadrupling of the price of oil in 1974 greatly increased the foreign trade imbalances of nearly all countries: trade surpluses, especially among oil-exporting countries, and trade deficits, notably among oil-importing countries, swelled, and were now intermediated by commercial international banks rather than, as previously, through the International Monetary Fund. When the international debt became excessive, when interest rates on that debt rose at the start of the 1980s, and as commodity prices started to fall, the scene was set for a major international banking crisis as governments in Mexico, Brazil, Poland and elsewhere announced that they could not service their foreign borrowing. The International Monetary Fund, that was called in to provide emergency assistance had insufficient resources. The US Government came under pressure from the major New York banks that dominated international banking, Citibank, J.P. Morgan, Chase Manhattan and others, to come up with a solution that would protect those banks from failure due to their excessive exposure to defaulting governments in the Third World.

An initial solution was put forward in October 1985 by James Baker, the US Treasury Secretary. This offered the rescheduling of debts owed by the fifteen most indebted governments, while requesting multilateral financial institutions, such as the IMF, and commercial international banks to lend more in order to facilitate the refinancing of indebted governments' foreign debts. The rescheduling was secured more or less by default. The IMF and the multilateral financial agencies lent as much as they could, under conditions that devastated the economies and polities of too many poor countries. This allowed the commercial international banks to escape the consequences of that default, which would have brought down those banks.

Nevertheless, the initiative failed. Like the recent policy initiatives to resolve the international debt crisis of 2007–2009, it treated the problem of excessive debt as merely the problem of liquidity that it appeared to be to bankers in the international financial markets (another reason why debt crises cannot be left to bankers to resolve). The crisis lingered on until 1989, when Baker's successor, Nicolas Brady, put forward his own solution, which involved refinancing through the issue of bonds backed by US Treasury bonds (the so-called Brady Bonds). But it also gave indebted governments the incentive to develop the domestic capital markets through which those governments could refinance more securely their foreign debts. The external debt of the most indebted governments was thus successfully 'hedged' with processes of capital market inflation that were set off by financial liberalisation in emerging markets. Again the problem of excessive debt was not resolved by introducing more liquidity into the system. But by the time 'emerging market crises' broke out from the mid-1990s onwards, the governments of those emerging markets were largely off the hook of their external debts.

The title article of this volume comes from the period in between the Baker and the Brady Initiatives. The immediate consequences of that article for my professional career proved to be enriching if only because they caused me to reflect upon why what I had written was so shocking. Some of these reflections inspired later work and the essays appearing in this volume, even if at the time of writing I was unaware of that inspiration.

The subsequent essays in this volume show how my ideas on finance have evolved since 1986, in part as my understanding of finance and its economics has deepened, but in part too as the financial edifice, whose construction started in the 1980s, has revealed cracks and subsidence problems culminating in the financial crisis of recent years. The essays were written to make more accessible some of the more technical economic analysis of my monographs and academic papers, as well as to indicate some of the social and political consequences of finance. These consequences were overlooked in the enthusiasm of financial planning and construction, and tend to be neglected even now. Today, critics of finance tend to populist recriminations, blaming bankers and financiers for their alleged excesses, instead of examining how the financial system could generate such extravagance in a profession noted for its conservatism, if not caution. In the Middle Ages, bad things were alleged to happen because 'evil is abroad'. Our understanding of banking and finance has greatly improved since that time. But when things go wrong it is still too easy to revert to such mystifications.

In the years that followed the publication of that article, I came to terms with the fact that, despite my initial conviction that the world economy was suffering from an excess of debt, the crash that was to eliminate that excess would periodically appear on the threshold, but never enter to take over the edifice of finance. In the course of writing my first book on finance, *The Economics of Financial Markets and the 1987 Crash*,[3] I realised that the resilience of the financial markets is due to a structural change in the relationship between finance and the real economy that came about with the shift to funded pension schemes during the 1970s and the 1980s. The more or less compulsory subscription to the financial markets entailed by such schemes was supposed to increase the amount of savings available for business investment. In practice the promised industrial renaissance failed to materialise. I worked out that this was because the inflow of credit into the financial markets, or financial inflation, made those markets themselves far more attractive and remunerative as vehicles for investment than the arduous business of making more lasting use-values. As I noted at the time, 'in an era of finance, finance mostly finances finance'.

The second section of the volume contains some of my essays on the Economics of Financial Inflation. It starts with an essay on 'Money in globalised times'. This was originally written in 2003 for an encyclopaedia of globalisation that changed editors so that my essay fell away along with the editor who commissioned it. At around the same time, I was invited by Alfredo Saad-Filho to contribute a chapter on International Finance to a volume edited by him and Deborah Johnston, *Neoliberalism: A Critical Reader* (Pluto Press 2005). In key respects my views on neo-liberalism, if not on international finance, have changed since writing that chapter. The version presented here represents my current views more comprehensively.

The third essay in this section, on Financial Innovation, emerged out of a re-reading of John Hobson's *Gold, Prices and Wages*. Hobson's critique scandalised John Maynard Keynes, who was reviewing it for the *Economic Journal*.[4] Keynes was outraged by Hobson's attack on the 'quantity theory of money' (the idea that inflation is caused by increases in the supply of money). Nevertheless, in Hobson's idea that credit expands through with the emergence of new financial assets, is a view of financial innovation that supports in a very appropriate way Keynes's later theory of liquidity preference, and illuminates the approach to financial innovation that was espoused by Hyman P. Minsky in his last writings. The essay published here is an extended version of a brief written for Oxford Analytica at the beginning of 2009.

The next two essays emerged out of entries that were contributed to a recent edition of the *International Encyclopaedia of the Social Sciences*. They examine the way in which non-financial firms accommodate financial inflation by expanding their balance sheets, through leverage and goodwill. The final two essays in this section bring the various preceding essays together to show how the phenomena described in those

Introduction

essays – credit, innovation and corporate finance – can constitute a process of financial inflation. The first essay was published in Spanish as 'Inflación en los Mercados Financieros' ('Financial Inflation') in E. Correa and A. Girón (eds.) *Economía Financiera Contemporánea* Mexico D.F.: Porrua, Las ciencas sociales, 2004, pp. 141–169. The second essay, 'Financial Inflation and Why It matters', is based on a brief for Oxford Analytica, that I have extended to show more precisely how financial inflation gives rise to crisis.

The second section of this volume discusses the culture of financial inflation. I have long argued that financial inflation gives rise to illusions about the financial markets. These illusions proliferate in particular among those who devote their time virtually exclusively to the study of the markets, either because of an overwhelming desire to 'make money' or because of a vicarious desire to rationalise such money-making. The first essay in this section reviews the evolution of finance theory over the second half of the twentieth century, from the attempt to understand the catastrophe of 1929 to the provision of mood music for financial inflation: reinforcing the commonplace insights and sales efforts of fund managers, and soothing the financial anxieties of the propertied classes. The essay is an extended version of my review of G. Poitras (ed.) *Pioneers of Financial Economics. Volume 2: Twentieth Century Contributions*. The review was published in *History of Economics Review* No. 49 Winter 2009, pp. 104–107. The second essay originated in a review, published in *History of Economics Review* No. 45 Winter 2007, pp. 127–131, of Perry Mehrling's *Fischer Black and the Revolutionary Idea of Finance*.

The remaining essays in this section are concerned with the broader social consequences of finance. The third essay, on economic inequality and asset inflation, first appeared in that hypermodern medium, the political blog, in political-finance. blogspot.com 11 February 2009. It examines the impact of financial inflation on social stratification. The fourth essay in the section examines in particular the peculiar culture of the propertied middle classes that has emerged from the process of financial inflation. It is an extended version of the final section of my paper 'The Economics and Culture of Financial Inflation', which appeared in *Competition and Change* Vol. 13 No. 2, June 2009, pp. 147–158. The present essay, with minor editorial changes, appeared in *Monthly Review* Vol. 62, No. 4, September 2010, pp. 10–15.

The final section of this volume consists of essays in which I have sought to explain the origin and mechanics of the current financial crisis. The first of them, 'Everything you need to know about the financial crisis but couldn't find out because the experts were explaining it', arose out of notes that I put together for various lectures to non-economists during 2008 and 2009, explaining how the crisis had arisen and its likely course. The second essay, on the limitations of financial stabilisation by central banks, appears to have been originally written around 2004 when I was reflecting on a more ambitious project about financial reform. It expands on the issue of central bank policy under financial inflation and in crisis that I touched upon in the title article. Neither of these two essays has been previously published. The third essay, on 'International Business and the Crisis', is a revised version of a paper which appeared in *Critical Perspectives on International Business* Vol. 5 No. 1/2, 2009, pp. 162–164. It is important because it explains the key mechanisms by which the banking crisis has become a crisis for the rest of the economy in so many countries. The final essay, on 'Developing Countries and the Crisis Transmission Mechanism', has also been revised since it first appeared as 'How the Global Crisis is transmitted to developing countries', *Development Viewpoint* Centre for Development Policy and Research, School of Oriental and African Studies, University of London, February 2009, No. 24. It emerged out of discussions in which I was involved at SOAS.

That title article of 1986 also introduced me to a number of individuals who shared my disquiet at the economic, social and political consequences of financial inflation. The essays in this small volume show how my ideas have evolved since I wrote that commentary, and are my own personal tribute to those individuals and the many friends who have engaged with the ideas that I started examining in 1986. Among them were Richard Hall, Zvi Schloss, Geoff Harcourt, Victoria Chick, Tadeusz Kowalik and others, who have in their turn guided me through some of the more obscure reflections on finance of Michał Kalecki, John Maynard Keynes, Joseph Schumpeter and Joseph Steindl. The effort to avoid default on my truly massive intellectual debts to these writers and friends has certainly improved my writing: it is not easy to discuss serious economic issues in an accessible way without being either trivial or patronising. Those giants of twentieth century economics could find broader audiences because they addressed crucial issues in a way that was engaged and, above all, honest. It is much more difficult to find such an audience when one is merely forecasting variables. The editors of the journals listed above have also contributed to refining and clarifying explanations that at times were somewhat too obvious to me. By and large, the papers that they published for me have been rewritten and now include additional reflections and observations. In addition, a large number of individuals have devoted a great deal of time and patience to discussing finance and financial crisis with me. They include Noemi Levy-Orlik, Sheila Dow, Gary Dymski, John Grahl, Murray Glickman, Charles Goodhart, John King, Photis Lysandrou, Marica Frangakis, Julio Lopez, Jo Michell, Juan Pablo Paschoa, Annina Kaltenbrunner, Radha Upadhyaya, Sanjay Krishnan, John Weeks, Tracy Mott, Anastasia Nesvetailova, Angelo Reati, Riccardo Bellofiore, Joseph Halevi, Robert Wade and Alessandro Vercelli. Their generosity absolves them of any responsibility for what remains of my errors. Jo Michell deserves especial thanks for assisting me in putting these essays into a consistent and publishable form.

Above all, these essays are a tribute to Anita Prażmowska, and Miriam Prażmowska-Toporowska, who was only weeks old when the title essay appeared. It is not possible adequately to express my profound gratitude for the support that they gave, for my sake and because they would not allow their own properly diminished respect for authority to stand in the way of speaking out where ignorance, injustice and oppression prevail.

Jan Toporowski
London
September 2010

'Not everyone is a debtor who wishes to be;
not everyone who wishes makes a creditor'
François Rabelais

1

Why the World Economy Needs a Financial Crash

An unrecognised merit of Rosa Luxemburg's *The Accumulation of Capital* (London Routledge and Kegan Paul, 1951) is that its theory of international finance is of startling relevance today.

In this book, which could still be read with profit by many City economists, Rosa Luxemburg analysed the process of capital accumulation (i.e. economic development) in colonial territories around the turn of the century. Lacking their own sources of finance, the major capital projects of those times were paid for by floating shares and stocks on the London Stock Exchange or international loans.

Inevitably, the engineers and sponsors of the development schemes tended to be over sanguine about their projects' future profitability. Too often costs exceeded projected expenses and initial borrowings proved insufficient, so that, even if completed, the projects were over-loaded with debt repayments and interest. Non-payment of these would precipitate a financial crisis on the part of both lenders and borrowers. The resulting crash would so devalue the claims of the lenders on the project as to enable it eventually to be completed, or continue in operation. In this way, many banks and financiers were ruined, but the projects themselves (like railway construction in Britain) were rarely altogether abandoned. Thus, the accumulation of capital proceeded, developing the relatively backward parts of the world and the developed countries themselves, using the money hoards of rentiers to pay for investment, and then defaulting to avoid meeting the claims of those rentiers.

Fortunately, since those times, another less catastrophic means of devaluing the claims of rentiers on economic development came to prevail. This was inflation, which devalued rentier claims, while tending to maintain the value of development projects and their revenues upon completion.

The relevance of all this to the Third Word debt crisis is immediately obvious. However, the old solution of ruining the rentiers (in this case the international banks and their creditors) no longer seems to be available. The position of the international banks is reinforced by central banks' implicit, if not explicit, willingness to act as lenders of last resort in order to avoid precisely that financial crash which would resolve the debt problem by devaluing it all. The banks themselves have reinforced their claims in the Third World by the use of floating rate interest, which has increased the value of interest charges since the 1970s. Moreover, by denominating their claims in currencies such as the US dollar and West German D-mark, that have tended to keep their value relative to commodities and other currencies, the banks have prevented their claims from being devalued by inflation.

Nevertheless, the decision of debtor countries such as Poland, Nigeria, Peru and Argentina to limit debt service payments to a minority share of their export earnings testifies to the urgent need of those countries to be released from the grip of rentier claims that are paralysing their trade and development. However, this solution is merely a way of easing the current payments problem by taking out more debt. Undiminished by devaluation, the acceleration in the growth of these claims must eventually crush either the rentiers, or the countries themselves.

There are three other possible solutions. One is the US Treasury Secretary James Baker's proposal to lend more money to debtor countries to enable them to maintain essential trade and minimise forced rescheduling.

Another solution is for real interest rates to fall drastically. While this could alleviate the problem somewhat, it is unlikely to come to pass. This is because of the way in which unregulated international markets operate, and the gradual integration into those markets of domestic financial markets in the OECD countries, a trend that the authorities in them seem powerless to reverse. Commercial banks operate in unregulated markets by drawing in funds whose supply is elastic, and directing them to borrowers whose demand for funds is relatively interest-inelastic. This enables banks to maximise their margins (until competition squeezes them out and forces banks to seek other relatively interest-inelastic borrowers). But it also tends to lever up interest rates in ostensibly free and competitive markets.

Both the Baker solution and lower interest rates are really ways of tinkering about with the problem, and offer solutions that at best will merely postpone the inevitable. A much more effective solution would be to devalue rentier claims by a short, sharp bout of inflation, preferably in the US.

However, in present circumstances, this is even less likely than lower interest rates, because of the stranglehold that deregulated financial markets are increasingly coming to have on government monetary policy in the OECD countries. Any government which appears even to tolerate inflation, let alone tries to engineer it, is increasingly likely to find its finances paralysed by financial markets and their dread of the systematic devaluation of their claims.

Thus the only practical conclusion that can be drawn under present circumstances is of the need for a financial crash. Obviously, such a crash would have an adverse effect on most of those in the City of London now preparing with enthusiasm for the Brave New Financial World after the 'Big Bang'. It would also temporarily dislocate much economic activity and have a disastrous effect on many whose incomes and wealth are based on financial assets. The Government policy, already over-dependent on the continuation of the present bull market through its reliance on asset sales to finance current expenditure, would also suffer a severe reverse in its attempts to promote services as an alternative to stagnating industrial activity. In addition, a financial crash would dramatically sour the attractions of a 'share-owning democracy' and make untenable the notion of private pension schemes as alternatives to state provision.

Those drawing their main incomes directly from City activities are relatively few. There are many more in Britain and abroad who would stand to gain from a revival of trade, investment and production which are currently suffering progressive paralysis from the burden of rentier claims. The devaluation of those claims is a necessary, if insufficient condition for the quickening of real economic activity and perhaps even the survival of the capitalist system.

PART I
The Economics of Financial Inflation

2

Money in Globalised Times

'Gladstone, speaking in a parliamentary debate on Sir Robert Peel's Bank Act of 1844 and 1845, observed that even love has not turned more men into fools than has meditation upon the meaning of money. He spoke of Britons to Britons. The Dutch, on the other hand, who in spite of Petty's doubts possessed a divine sense for money speculation from time immemorial, have never lost their senses in speculation about money.'
K. Marx, *A Contribution to the Critique of Political Economy*, New York: International Publishers 1970, p.64

Modern finance is about 'convenience money', that is, having a store of liquid assets that allows firms and households to meet unplanned expenditures, or unexpected declines in income, without the bother of having to sell possessions (labour or inanimate property) or borrow in an emergency. Such convenience money is part of accumulated wealth. As globalisation has linked up local and national markets for wealth, so too it has changed the kind of money that we use.

As every textbook reminds us, to the point of tedium, money is a social convention which makes trade easier because prices are set in amounts of the money-commodity ('unit of account'), and because the proceeds from selling commodities may be held as money until the desired commodity comes into the market ('store of value'). Under capitalism, financial markets concentrate large amounts of money (savings, or 'interest-bearing capital' in Marx) which can then be used to finance trade and production, in exchange for a portion of the profit from that trade or production. Since the twentieth century, such money capital is mostly used to generate profit from operations in financial markets, buying financial assets and selling them later at a higher price. Money therefore has primarily followed the development of trade and

9

the expansion of markets. In recent times, however, movements of money capital in and out of different currencies has disturbed the effectiveness of money in facilitating trade.

The Evolution of Money

Before the nineteenth century, when markets were mostly local and small, locally produced coins were adequate for the needs of trade. In the great trading basins of the Mediterranean or navigable rivers such as the Volga or the Danube and elsewhere, as markets became more integrated, coins minted in different trading cities, each with different values, circulated alongside each other. The practical need to be able to calculate their value in terms of each other was resolved by valuing them according to the amount of precious metals (gold or silver) contained in the coins. A coin containing twelve ounces of gold was considered double the value of one containing six ounces of gold. Establishing the proper relative value of gold in relation to silver was more difficult.

In 1717, faced with a shortage of silver coinage for English trade, the ratio of silver to gold was fixed on the recommendation of the Master of the Mint, Sir Isaac Newton, by Crown proclamation at 21 silver shillings to the gold guinea. But this over-valued gold to such an extent that, for the next century, hardly any silver was brought to the London Mint for coining. Britain in effect went onto a gold standard. Nevertheless, at the end of the nineteenth century there were many serious monetary economists, such as Alfred Marshall, who advocated the return to the use of gold and silver currency, or bimetallism, if only because Britain's most important colony, India, remained on a silver standard until 1893.

As international trade developed in the eighteenth century, paper claims, and bills of exchange came to be used for payment. These had the advantage over coins or bullion (bars of precious metal) that they were more secure, and afforded possibilities of delayed payment, that is credit. The person who received such a bill in delayed payment could always bring forward its payment by selling it at a discount, that is at less than its value on maturity, to one of the banks specialising in this discount trade in London, Amsterdam or New York. From this emerged paper money, issued by local banks to reduce the circulation of gold in circumstances where the security of gold held in public hands was always precarious. However, by the middle of the nineteenth century it was considered prudent by most respectable bankers and economists that issuers of paper money should only put into circulation as much paper money as they had gold. Otherwise, it was feared that by increasing the amount of currency available to buy goods, an unlimited issue of paper money would give rise to inflation and speculation, or profiteering from the increases in prices of goods or property. Such inflation and speculation occurred in the United States after independence, in France after the 1789 Revolution, and in Britain during the Napoleonic Wars.

Gradually, paper money and coins of precious and industrial metals replaced gold in domestic circulation in more or less standardised units: pounds shillings and pence in Britain, dollars and cents in the US. But, like a dim echo of the times when coins issued by different mints circulated alongside each other, the gold 'content', or value against gold, of domestic currencies was supposed to represent their international value. This is what was meant by the gold standard, which most wealthier countries adopted after 1870. Under this system, trade and finance flourished. This apparent prosperity had nothing to do with any intrinsic qualities of gold, but everything to do with the ease with which international payments could be made with claims against accounts held in financial centres. There, claims, on being presented, would be paid with paper money such as Bank of England pound notes that were convertible into gold.

Indeed, the system even had its apparently bizarre but rational aspects: the Tsarist government of Russia would ship gold to a particular financial centre, such as Paris, for example. Increased gold reserves made banks lower interest rates in order to encourage borrowing. The Russian government would then raise a loan at the lower rate of interest, before taking its gold off to another financial centre, where it would raise another loan made cheap by the influx of Russian gold. In the 1920s the British Treasury official, Sir Ralph Hawtrey argued that a shipload of gold bullion should be sent New York in order to cause the US dollar to appreciate in the foreign exchange markets against sterling.

Bretton Woods

Inevitably, the whole system collapsed under the weight of debts contracted under it because of its apparent 'soundness', as well as those debts contracted to pay for the First World War. By the 1930s, the inability to make international payments and capital transfers of a stable value was irrevocably associated with economic depression. Economists since then have not ceased to argue about what it was precisely that governments did wrong to bring this catastrophe upon their citizens. The Great Depression of the 1930s confirmed a belief, among even the most practical bankers and financiers, in a 'natural' order in which cross-border payments and capital transfers can be made easily and at minimum cost throughout the world. By implication, the only obstacles to the unrestricted flows of international money are supposed to be politically inspired regulations: the national (or state, in the US) jurisdictions that have replaced brute force in securing commercial or financial claims.

It was in this context that the statesmen and economists gathered at Bretton Woods in the United States in 1944 to reconstruct an international trading and financial system. Most of them had the gold standard in the back of their minds as their bench-mark for their task. However, the US by then had over eighty-percent of the capitalist world's gold reserves, much of it delivered in payment for Wartime support or as security on loans. They agreed on an indirect gold standard, in which all other currencies were to be convertible at a fixed rate against the US dollar, and that dollar was made convertible against gold at a fixed rate of US$35 per fine ounce.

In order to keep to their fixed exchange rates, most governments limited access to foreign currency by residents of their countries. By obliging residents to exchange their foreign currency for domestic currency, central banks could obtain more foreign currency with which to intervene in the foreign exchange market. In addition, foreign capital transfers were limited, and foreign exchange to buy imports was often rationed. In London, and subsequently in Hong Kong and Singapore, free markets in foreign currency emerged. But these provided payments and transfer facilities mostly for multinational companies and international banks.

In any case, the system was bound to fail. Under the Bretton Woods system the US could pay for its balance of payments deficits by issuing dollars. These dollars were permanently in demand as foreign currency reserves for banks in other countries. The dollars that were returned for exchange in the US for gold merely drained gold from the United States. On August 15, 1971, the US government ceased the sale of gold from its reserves on demand.

Free Markets and Globalisation

In the 1970s the world moved to a system in which various currencies circulated alongside each other in free markets, operating in London and Singapore for example, but accessible only to non-residents of those countries. Most governments still restricted the foreign exchange transactions of their residents by capital controls; that is, through the regulation of cross-border payments and capital transfers. The absence of any intrinsic common feature against which to measure their value, now that gold was no longer in use, meant that since the 1970s the exchange value of currencies has increasingly been determined in foreign currency markets, more or less beyond government control. This made capital controls, i.e., the regulation of cross-border payments and capital transfers, increasingly easy to evade. In the 1970s, the governments of the United States of America and the United Kingdom eliminated these controls, making it much more difficult for other countries to keep their foreign exchange markets stable. Effectively the two countries with the largest credit-creation capacity could now throw unlimited dollar or sterling credit into other countries' foreign exchange markets. Western European countries deregulated cross-border capital flows at the beginning of the 1990s, ostensibly in preparation for European monetary union.

By the start of the twenty-first century, in the most advanced capitalist countries in North America and Western Europe, bank credits and debits replaced paper money or coins for all but the smallest transactions. Bank regulations against money laundering, making it difficult to pay large amounts of cash into or out of bank accounts, are now extending the use of bank credit to the less advanced capitalist countries and the newly industrialised countries, because payments by bank credit, unlike payments using notes and coins, can be traced. This provides reliable and secure mechanisms for payments and capital transfers inside particular countries. Cross-border payments and transfers are less reliable because exchange rates between currencies are now freely determined by currency markets, so that the value of a payment or transfer may vary from day to day. In addition, most countries, in particular the poorer and less developed ones, still operate controls on their residents' purchases and sales of foreign currency.

The money that is used today therefore varies in its effectiveness. At one extreme, the money that is used in poorer and less developed countries is subject to fluctuations in value because of price inflation and deflation. Periodically such money is disturbed by banking crises or foreign exchange crises because the governments of those countries, and their central banks, cannot keep their currencies convertible in a stable way against currencies issued by other governments and central banks. At the other extreme, the money of the most financially advanced countries is more or less stable in value. Because there is more or less a permanent demand for it abroad, it is easier to use for international payments and hence to keep it convertible against other currencies. This permanent foreign demand for the money of the financially advanced countries results arises not only because these countries are rich and powerful. Mostly this permanent foreign demand for their currencies occurs because the financially advanced countries have well developed financial markets, in which holders of their currencies can buy a wide range of financial assets. This additional, internal convertibility of the currencies of financially advanced countries makes them more internationally desirable. Buying such a currency gives access to a much wider range of financial investments than is available for the currencies of poorer, financially less sophisticated countries.

Such differences in the possibilities for gainful investment of different currencies tend to destabilise currencies and rob them of their effectiveness as money. Broadly, three strategies have been adopted by various governments to stabilise their currencies. The first is a drive among less financially advanced countries to develop financial markets in the image and likeness of those of the most financially advanced country, the United States of America. Some governments of small countries, such as Switzerland or Hong Kong, manage to keep stable currencies because in effect they offer discreet, less regulated, banking facilities for residents of other countries who can evade financial regulations by keeping their money in such 'off-shore' financial centres. Such centres benefit from a parasitic relationship with the wealth and regulation of other countries.

In other countries in Latin America, Africa, or the Pacific Basin, governments try to develop banking, business and political links with more financially advanced countries as a way of stabilising their currencies. However, for this to work properly, it requires guarantees of automatic support from the central bank in the country to whose currency the poorer government is trying to link its money. This works in, for example, the poorer countries of the Franc Zone, mostly in sub-Saharan Africa, where governments have adopted a currency linked to the French Franc (now the Euro). But this link is at the cost of such a strict oversight of their government finances and financial systems that those countries have largely been left poor and economically backward. The spectacular collapse of the Argentine financial system in 2001, and the replacement of its currency that had been tied to the US dollar by various formal and informal alternative currencies, provides an excellent illustration of what can go wrong if such automatic support from the more advanced country's central bank is not forthcoming.

The third way of introducing a currency that can be effectively used at home and abroad is a formal monetary union, in which governments agree to share the use of a common currency as money. The most notable example of this in recent times is the European Monetary Union, which now covers a majority of Western European countries. Its geographic size allows the Union to span a range of countries and industries which makes the external use of its currency, the Euro, largely unnecessary for residents of the Euro area. (The Euro is used outside the Union mostly to buy oil and raw material imports, some manufactured goods, and to pay for capital exports.) It also has the potential to concentrate financial activities in centres, which can then offer the range of financial assets that would create a permanent demand for the Euro in international currency markets. However, the financial conditions for membership of the European Monetary Union encourage governments to operate with financial surpluses, taking money out of the economy and preventing governments from running significant budget deficits if the economy is in recession. This reduces the political advantages of the Union, as well as the scope for developing European financial markets: historically, a broad market in government securities has been the foundation for markets in private sector securities.

In a financially interdependent world, only the largest and most financially advanced countries can secure a stable currency for themselves. This stability is obtained by exaggerating the influence of the financial markets, whose poor judgement is readily supported by backward-looking politicians and economists with a nostalgia for the apparently free international money markets of the gold standard. Now that our money is mostly credit, more enlightened international co-operation is needed to make the interdependent monetary systems of the world work properly.

3

Neo-Liberalism and International Finance

Cross-border credit and money capital transfers, and international money in the sense of cross-border payments, have always played a key role in the worldview of economic liberalism. Frequently international money and financial activity have been regarded as proving that, without any government or social direction, trade can reach all corners of the globe and foster capitalist business enterprise everywhere. Behind this view is a nostalgia for the era of the gold standard, approximately between 1870 and 1914, when world currencies were convertible into gold at a fixed rate. The breakdown of that system during the First World War was associated with suspensions of international payments and capital flows. Its return in 1925 was welcomed by Oliver Sprague, adviser to the US Government and the Bank of England, in the following terms:

> This return to the haven of familiar monetary practice is significant of the widespread conviction that the gold standard is an essential factor in the maintenance of a reasonable measure of international stability, for which there is no practicable substitute.[1]

Financial instability had come to be associated with the absence of a gold standard for money and exchange rates. Such instability gave rise to and continues to foster the delusion that the international financial system can provide an automatic mechanism to deal with economic problems. As the National Bureau of Economic Research in New York reported in 1940:

> Before 1925 concentration upon the goal of a return to normal and upon the achievement of stable exchange rates,

and after 1925 the splendours of a stable exchange rate blinded the eyes of bankers and of the world in general. The illusion that the economic maladjustments would be corrected by automatic forces was dominant in the world's financial thinking.[2]

International finance remains crucial to the neo-liberal project of a capitalism in which any imbalances are spontaneously eliminated by market forces that make supply equal to demand. Any financial instability is blamed on imperfections in the national or international financial system that may be remedied without challenging the capitalist system. In our time this is a view that has re-emerged following the dismantling of the Keynesian system of 'big government' and economic stabilisation policies. In the decades after the Second World War, when governments tried to steer the economy using various direct and indirect controls, apologists for laissez-faire capitalism argued that such Keynesian policies were undermining economic stability and capitalist enterprise. Today governments subordinate their economic policies to promoting business and finance.[3] The increased economic instability that followed the abandoning of Keynesian stabilisation policies requires both an explanation of that instability and some alternative measures of promoting stability. The system of international finance offers an obvious source of economic disturbances and a target for the reforming zeal of those apologists for capitalism who cling to the 'gold standard' belief – that there is some set of international monetary and financial arrangements under which the problems of capitalism will be automatically resolved by market forces.

It should be emphasised that Keynesian stabilisation policies were not abandoned for purely ideological reasons; i.e., because, as many critics of neo-liberalism argue, a lasser-faire animus spread from Chicago, infecting politicians of all parties and persuading them of the benefits of free markets. In fact Keynesianism never worked very well and, in particular, Keynesian systems of financial regulation (capital controls and managed exchange rates) could not withstand the growing pools of unregulated international credit, the Euromarkets (see below), which came to dominate international finance. The last major attempt to engineer Keynesian counter-cyclical policy, that of President François Mitterand in France in 1980, proved almost completely ineffective. An alternative to Keynesianism was needed. For its ideologues, neo-liberalism was a dogmatic belief in free market forces. For most politicians and economic policy-makers, it was simply a belief, born out of the failures of Keynesianism in the 1970s, that free markets could not be resisted.

The Rise of International Finance

As the Second World War came to an end, the political leaders of the Western Allies sought a 'return to the haven of familiar monetary practice' at the inter-governmental economic conference that was held in Bretton Woods in the US in 1944. But by then there was no possibility of any return to the gold standard. Central banks without gold reserves could not return to the gold standard, and over four fifths of the gold outside the Soviet Union was in the US. The result of the Bretton Woods deliberations was an indirect gold standard: central banks and their governments were obliged to maintain fixed exchange rates against the US dollar while the Federal Reserve Bank of New York was given the responsibility of keeping the US dollar convertible for gold at a rate of US$35 per fine ounce of gold. The International Monetary Fund (IMF) was set up to police the system of fixed exchange rates. Governments were not allowed to change the exchange rate of their currency without the IMF's approval. If a central bank was running out of gold or dollars with which to maintain their fixed exchange rate, then the IMF would lend dollars under increasingly strict conditions. The World Bank was also set up at Bretton Woods to finance the reconstruction of countries devastated by the War, and subsequently to finance the economic development of poorer countries.

From this period dates the hegemony of the US dollar in international finance. This was the currency for which all other currencies and assets could be bought virtually anywhere in the world. Every other currency was good for payments in the country in which it was issued, but was less acceptable outside that country. However, the exchange rate stability was not sustainable. Through the 1940s and the 1950s, the United States had balance of payments deficits averaging over a billion dollars per year. These dollars rarely returned to the US to buy US goods or financial assets: US interest rates were low, and the status of the dollar as a reserve currency meant that any bank abroad was willing to hold that currency. This gave the United States a unique privilege of 'seigniorage': its residents could pay for their excess imports with dollars as if conveniently printed for them by the Federal Reserve system. Actual trade payments are made by bank credit, so it was really the banking system that was expanding dollar deposits held by exporters abroad. Virtually every other country had to keep its demand for imports under control by deflationary demand management in order not to run out of foreign currency to pay for imports. US intervention in Korea and Taiwan, followed by its costly war in Vietnam, added to the steady outflow of dollars.

The dollars held outside the United States were principally held in unofficial and unregulated dollar markets that emerged first in London in 1957 and then in Singapore. Interest rates in these markets were considerably higher than the regulated ones in the US. This made it even more attractive to deposit dollars in these 'Euromarkets', whose principal banks were in any case American. Borrowers also found it convenient to borrow from them, because they did not have to submit to central bank regulations over foreign currency borrowing. Such regulation was an important part of the way in which central banks kept to the exchange rates fixed at Bretton Woods. Residents of a country were obliged to exchange their foreign currency for domestic currency. In this way, the foreign currency in a country would be concentrated in the central bank, which could use this foreign exchange as part of the bank's exchange rate management. Governments in particular found that they could borrow from the Euromarkets with fewer questions asked than they could from the International Monetary Fund. The Euromarkets then spawned smaller markets in other 'Eurocurrencies' held 'off-shore', or outside their country of issue, and a Eurocurrency bond market.

Some of the dollar outflow did return and was exchanged for gold, so that these decades were also marked by a steady outflow of gold reserves from the US. By 1970 it was clear that the US was having difficulty in maintaining dollar convertibility against gold at the rate fixed in Bretton Woods. In 1971 the US Government suspended gold payments. In 1973 fixed exchange rates were abandoned.

Problems of International Finance

After the breakdown of the Bretton Woods system in 1971, the main capitalist economies were plunged into inflationary recessions that were dubbed 'stagflation'. Raw materials prices rose sharply, most notably the price of crude oil, which quadrupled between 1973 and 1976. Developing countries suddenly experienced huge export surpluses (if they were lightly populated and had an expensive commodity like oil to export), or were plunged into trade deficits if they were oil importers. The enlarged export revenues, in particular of the oil exporting countries, found their way into the Euromarkets. There, the principal borrowers were now those countries with unsustainable trade deficits. It could only be a matter of time before this 'recycling' of export surpluses, through the international banking system to countries with chronic trade deficits, broke down in a debt crisis.

In December 1982, the Government of Mexico, followed rapidly by the Governments of Brazil, Argentina and Poland, declared that it was unable to meet its foreign debt payments. (Domestic debt is always an easier matter, because Governments can issue new debt, raise taxes or take credits from their central bank to repay domestic debt.) Left to market forces, the banks which lent to them would have become insolvent and collapsed. Once the debt had been 'eliminated' in this way, more prudent international borrowing from the surviving banks would have eventually resumed. However, while economic liberals applauded the enterprise of predominantly American international banks during the 1970s in inflating international debt, the market-loving government of the US President Ronald Reagan shrank from allowing the market to have its way with those banks during the 1980s. Not for the first time, the failure of US banks during the 1930s depression was used to conjure up economic catastrophes that would result from 'systemic failure' if the American international banks were allowed to collapse.

The IMF, which had been marginalised during the 1970s by the collapse of fixed exchange rates and the ease with which governments could borrow from the Euromarkets, now came into its own again. Its new function was to rehabilitate the predominantly American international banking system by refinancing the debts of governments that had borrowed from it.[4] The price of that refinancing was a severely deflationary financial stabilisation package known as Structural Adjustment. This was ostensibly voluntary, but governments applying for loans knew what would secure the approval of the IMF. An appeal to international banks to lend more, the Baker Initiative in 1986, failed: most bankers were sufficiently worldly to realise that lending more money to governments that could not repay existing debt was imprudent, to say the least.

The Brady Initiative in 1989 was more successful. This involved exchanging foreign bank debt for bonds secured on US government bonds, with some reduction in the value of that debt. The involvement of the US Treasury in guaranteeing those Brady bonds was, depending on your point of view, indicative of the responsibility that the American Government now took for the stability of the international financial system, or symptomatic of the way in which international finance had been taken over by US interests. Either way, it was not particularly neo-liberal, with the US Treasury and the IMF organising the refinancing of US banks by refinancing the governments that owed money that could not be repaid to those banks. Their commitment to this refinancing contrasts with the draconian purges recommended and imposed on foreign banks during the 1990s in the wake of emerging market crises.[5]

Stabilisation of International Finance

The Brady Initiative owed its success to the inflation of markets for long-term securities that was a notable feature of financial developments in Japan (until 1991), the United States and the United Kingdom during the 1980s and the 1990s. This made it easy and relatively inexpensive to sell long-term bonds into the capital markets of those countries in order to refinance banks and indebted governments. Such inflation of long-term securities markets had two consequences. First of all, the Bank for International Settlements, under the Basle Accord of 1989, was able to impose additional capital requirements, which banks were supposed to hold against their more risky foreign assets or loans. Banks with access to liquid capital markets were able relatively easily to raise the additional capital requirements.

The second effect of rising (i.e., liquid) capital markets in North America and the UK was that other governments sought to engineer such markets in their own countries. This would offer governments in developing or newly industrialised countries the possibility of issuing debt domestically, which was easier to manage and repay because it was in local currency. Such financial development had already been envisaged under the 'structural adjustment' policies imposed on indebted governments during the 1980s. The theory behind 'structural adjustment' was that private enterprise would naturally flourish in the absence of government regulation. However, expanding private enterprise requires financial resources. This brought financial liberalisation, or 'financial deepening', as its advocates call it, to the forefront of the neo-liberal agenda as a way of mobilising domestic saving for private investment, and as a way of augmenting domestic saving with foreign savings.

Financial liberalisation was promoted by removing controls on capital movements into and out of countries, and encouraging money centre and stock market activities in developing and newly industrialised countries. Domestic money inflows were secured by directing pension contributions into these markets. Once the stock market was rising, foreign portfolio investment was attracted by the possibilities of speculative gains. This brought in foreign money capital, whose conversion into local currency helped to stabilise its exchange rate. Such markets in developing and newly-industrialised countries were called 'emerging markets', to denote their emergence from backwardness and government control ('financial repression ') into the orbit of the modern, rational and enlightened market forces of international finance.

However, capital inflows into emerging markets could flow out even more quickly than they had come in. In particular, financial inflation and any investment boom arising out of it increased prodigiously the demand for imports into an emerging market country. Higher imports then increased further the amount of capital inflow that was needed to keep the exchange rate stable. If the exchange rate fell, then this would devalue the assets of foreign capital holders (principally investment funds based in North America and Western Europe). Any threat of such a devaluation could cause capital to flee an emerging market in advance of such a devaluation. Such devaluations were in fact inevitable, and caused financial markets to crash in Mexico in 1995, in East Asia in 1997, in Russia in 1998, in Turkey 2001, and in Argentina in 2002.[6]

As a general rule of thumb, each crisis from the international debt crisis in 1982 to the Russian crisis of 1998 cost twice as much to refinance as the previous one; so that the 1995 Mexican crisis cost twice as much as the 1982 debt crisis to resolve; the 1997 East Asian Crisis cost twice as much as the Mexican crisis to settle; and the Russian crisis cost twice as much as the East Asian Crisis. This escalation in the expense of avoiding the collapse of international banks and investment funds has been borne largely by the International Monetary Fund and the people of emerging market countries. The IMF has had to lend money to governments of emerging market countries, while the people in those countries have had to put up with the economic recession and degradation of public services that were the price of IMF assistance. By the mid-1990s it was clear that this situation was not sustainable, if only because the US government provides nearly 40 per cent of IMF resources, and was thus obliged to put more and more money into securing international financial stability.

To limit its financial commitments, the IMF moved at the end of the 1990s to a system of selective automatic assistance to governments. The IMF now reports on the financial stability of its member governments, and only those with 'robust' financial systems can expect support from the Fund. However, emerging market governments are aware of the influence that American international banks have in Washington. Keeping such banks operating in an emerging market is therefore an insurance policy that secures support in Washington in the event that the emerging market experiences a crisis. In this way, the IMF was eventually and reluctantly induced to help Argentina in 2002.

Conclusion

Economic liberals believe that the unfettered pursuit of private gain can be kept in check and turned to the general social and economic benefit by naturally occurring market forces. This doctrine overlooks the political and social power that financial wealth bestows, a power that became apparent when this doctrine was applied to international finance. Far from being rational and transparent, as the advocates of financial liberalisation had wanted, the system remains corrupt, opaque and dependent on state support. Only the beneficiaries of the corruption have changed. Previously, petty bureaucrats in poor countries channelled scarce financial resources to their favourite projects. Now, with international bankers and fund managers and the state supporting them, the US Government and its allies channel finance to pro-American governments and companies they favour. At the same time stability has not been secured: selective assistance to countries with 'sound' financial systems simply means that the IMF will not help if a crisis arises unless that crisis happens to be in a country that has friends in Washington.

Critics of international finance have made various proposals to stabilise the system and make it more appropriate to the purposes of economic and social development. The most common suggestion has been a return to the cross-border capital controls that existed during the 1940s and the 1950s. Such controls, in many cases, were not eliminated until the 1990s. However, international bank deposits and financial assets held abroad are now so large that it would be difficult to enforce such controls. Indeed, the main reason for getting rid of such regulations was precisely because they could not be enforced.

Among the most famous stabilisation measures suggested has been a Tobin Tax, put forward by the distinguished American Keynesian James Tobin during the 1970s as a way of stabilising exchange rates. This would be a tax of between half and one per cent on every foreign exchange transaction. Recent proponents of this tax have suggested putting its proceeds to finance development projects in poor countries. This has genuinely popular support among activists who campaign for a more just international order. However, critics like the American Post-Keynesian Paul Davidson have argued that it would be ineffectual compared to the scale of the instability affecting the international financial markets. The Scottish economist John Grahl has argued that it would simply make it more difficult to develop financial markets outside the United States.[7] The Cambridge Keynesian Geoffrey Harcourt has advocated a tax on speculation. There is no doubt that the funds raised from such taxes could finance major social and economic improvements. But from the point of view of financial stabilisation, there is no evidence that such taxes would eliminate speculation. It could make markets even more unstable if it concentrates speculation where the expected return is highest. This author has argued that central banks should regulate financial markets more effectively by buying and selling securities to balance speculative selling or buying[8]. But this would need a major change in the way in which central banks operate.

For the citizen of a developing country – experiencing poverty, under-employment, and the collapse of the social fabric of her or his society and polity because her or his government is being turned into a debt collector for foreign banking and financial interests – it will be of little comfort to know that the system also degrades the economic, if not the social, fabric of the countries of its principal beneficiaries. The US and the UK, whose financial systems have been most inflated by laissez-faire finance supported by compulsory subscriptions to funded pension schemes, have slow industrial growth and employment. Their poor investment record belies the conventional wisdom of financial neo-liberals, that the best way to encourage real investment is to entrust even more money to an investment banker or international fund manager. However, as long as there are speculative gains to be made from the markets, there will be powerful interests opposing the international co-operation required to reform the system and make it more efficient.

4

Financial Innovation: Better Machines for Financial Inflation?

Many economists, bankers and policy-makers like to think of financial innovation as something like the innovation that occurs in engineering, consumer goods, or public services: an endless process of improving the quality or decreasing the cost of the goods and services that we enjoy. However, the financial crisis has cast a shadow over recent financial innovations, in particular those that claim to eliminate risk. The apparent failure of innovations such as credit default swaps, or credit insurance, has put into doubt the usefulness of financial innovations. The development of new financial instruments, in particular financial derivatives, was such a notable feature of the long financial boom from the end of the 1970s that financial innovation came to be associated with financial expansion, just as it is now associated with opaque credit devices of dubious value. Well-known figures in the world of finance, such as George Soros and Warren Buffett, have denounced financial derivatives. As the policy debate turns to the reregulation of the financial markets, the functions and social use-value of financial novelty is under scrutiny.

In their hey-day, the purveyors of financial innovations liked to advertise themselves as engineers, namely highly educated practical men (for they were almost universally men) who could design better machines or constructions. In fact, machines usually have a useful function, whereas financial innovations have negligible or no intrinsic use-value to anyone outside the financial markets. (This will be disputed by anyone who has ever used a credit card to push back a lock or cut a cake, although these are functions for which credit cards were not really designed.) Actually, financial innovation is an endogenous process within financial markets, internally generated in those markets as their activity develops and expands. As a process, financial innovation is not, as some have maintained, a response to policy or regulation from outside the markets, although particular financial instruments may be designed to evade regulation, or in response to government fiscal or monetary policy.

A simple definition of financial innovation is that it involves the invention and use of new financial instruments (for example, credit cards in the 1970s) or new uses for older instruments (e.g., using mobile telephones to make cross-border payments). This may be true, but it confuses the general appearance of innovations with their specific functions. Such a definition may be congenial to financial 'engineers' who would like to think of their activity as a truly creative activity endowing humanity with better machines. But it gives no indication of why such innovations come about.

In practice, financial innovations come about in three stages, each of them containing a different kind of innovation, and each one leading on to the next stage. By the time the final stage is reached it is possible that the three different kinds of innovation may be occurring simultaneously. But they are of a different kind nevertheless. Financial innovation starts in societies that have money and wealth, with that wealth being unequally distributed – an equal distribution of wealth is a major disincentive to financial innovation because it removes much of the desire to accumulate more wealth that arises from invidious comparison. Money can, of course, be used to buy goods and services, but wealth can only be enjoyed or applied productively. This situation gives rise to monetary innovation, i.e., the development of new forms of money. Examples of this abound in history. In the hey-day of the Roman Empire, landowners needed to be able to borrow to maintain a life-style in Rome or just tide them over a period of low agricultural prices. The mortgage, a loan secured originally on land, was developed to ease the financial plight of the landowners. Needless to say, once such a credit arrangement was available, it gave rise to a market in land simply by allowing its purchase without the need for prior saving. Land-banks, offering mortgages, were organised with similar effect by the colonial government of Kenya in the 1930s to ease the plight of the European settlers whose incomes were reduced by low commodity prices.[1]

Thus monetary innovation facilitated the emergence of asset markets. The most important phase of credit innovation in recent history came with the building of modern infrastructure and capitalist production on a large scale. The credit required to finance infrastructure and large-scale production far exceeded the credit which merchants were wont to draw on to finance cargoes and transportation of those cargoes. Hence the emergence of stocks and bonds, in particular from the second half of the nineteenth century, after Companies Acts were passed in most countries facilitating the setting up of companies that could issue stocks and shares.

Company stocks and shares joined a particular class of wealth which had existed since the seventeenth century, namely financial assets. The development of new financial assets or wealth is a second stage, or type of financial innovation. Such assets were pioneered centuries ago by Governments which needed to borrow money, usually to defray the costs of wars. Since medieval times, kings and princes had borrowed money from banks or even private individuals. But in the seventeenth century they developed a new instrument, namely annuities, which were sold to individuals who would pay to receive an income for the lifetime of a specified individual. Annuities were claims on Governments, but they were difficult to value since they depended on the expected life span of the beneficiary. By contrast, bonds had a fixed repayment value as well as a specified term. These were much more marketable assets. The introduction of such assets marks the second stage or type of financial innovation. Moreover, the marketability of financial assets in general gave rise to considerable credit innovation. A notorious and pioneering example of such innovation was John Law's scheme, in the first decades of the eighteenth century, for bank credit to finance the buying of shares in his French Mississippi Company, and the equivalent in Britain, the South Sea Company. He also pioneered the share option, and the ventures themselves were a prototype of the privatisations of state companies that became so common after the 1980s. The collapse of Law's companies may have set back the progress of credit innovation for a century and a half. But it certainly revealed the part that financial innovation plays in cycles of boom and bust in financial markets.

The proliferation of financial assets from the late-nineteenth-century onwards in the form of shares, loan stocks, debentures, preference shares and so on, greatly extended the possibilities for credit innovation. It became common now for banks to give credit against financial securities as well as against marketable physical assets. The possibility of being able to borrow against the security of financial assets was an important factor in the willingness of wealthy individuals to hold long-term financial assets. Borrowing against them allowed their owners to covert such assets, however temporarily, into credit without having to wait for bonds to be repaid, or find someone to buy them. On the one hand this eventually undermined the gold standard, because credit expanded to the point where the banknotes into which it could be converted exceeded gold reserves by a large margin. On the other hand it also gave rise to instability in those markets because any increased demand for an asset that caused its price to go up would then be followed by borrowing to buy that asset in order to obtain a speculative profit as it rose in value. The additional buying would cause the price of the asset to rise even further. If the price of an asset fell, then lenders would find that the quality of their collateral was reduced: a loan secured on a financial asset was less likely to be covered by the value of that asset. Banks would then demand more collateral, raise interest rates, or demand repayment of loans. These tended to cause selling of assets, which would make their prices fall even further.

Once asset prices started becoming unstable, the third stage or type of financial innovation emerged: namely, financial derivatives. These range from difference contracts (commitments to pay the difference between a price specified in the contract, called the 'strike' price, and the market price at a given time in the future or over a given period) to formal commitments to buy or sell the asset at a fixed price in the future ('call' or 'put' contracts as they are called in the futures business). Such contracts had been noted as early as the period of the South Sea Bubble, as incidental arrangements between individuals. But derivatives multiplied on the fringes of the huge expansion of financial asset markets in the second half of the nineteenth century, leading to the emergence of markets in which 'call' and 'put' contracts could be bought and sold. Once markets in financial derivatives were established, those derivatives became financial assets, however ephemeral, in their own right.

Already during the 1890s there was a lively debate among economists, bankers and policy-makers as whether and how this last kind of financial innovation should be regulated. The proponents of financial innovation and the financial firms that were selling them argued that, in return for relatively modest fees, they were providing a public service in offering industrial and commercial firms and professional investors a way of fixing the prices of various assets, including industrial and agricultural raw materials, thus providing certainty in an uncertain world.[2]

The opponents of derivatives saw them as simply a more sophisticated form of gambling which could ruin the otherwise sound finances of individuals and firms. Like any other kind of gambling, they argued that it should be strictly controlled. The advocates of these innovations presented them as forms of insurance. The more of it that people had, the more financially stable their lives would be. Any losses sustained on such contracts arose because they were not 'managed' properly. With the right advice from experts in the markets, derivatives were beneficial. As in the 1970s, the advocates won. They had a major practical advantage: asset markets were and are unstable. Money could be made out of that instability using financial derivatives, and no one has yet invented a foolproof way to prevent people with money from using it to make even more money no matter how ruinous the consequences may be for society. (Pyramid banking, for example, is banned virtually everywhere, but Bernard Madoff's scheme ran for years in the US.)

The current cycle of financial innovation starts with the 1930s Depression and the Second World War. The former wrecked, or at least severely curtailed, financial activities while the financing needs of the War required strict control of credit and flooded the markets with government debt whose markets needed to be closely managed. Again, monetary innovation led more general financial innovation with the rise of unregulated Euro-dollar balances in banks in London and Singapore. These in turn undermined the stability of asset markets, most notably in the case of foreign exchange markets where central banks had been charged under the Bretton Woods agreements to maintain fixed prices for US dollars.

The Euro-dollar markets spun off a variety of new financial instruments, from syndicated lending to Euro-currency bonds and securities. With the breakdown of fixed exchange rates, in the early 1970s, the process entered the third stage of innovation, with the proliferation of financial futures and derivatives. Here Milton Friedman, as a consultant to the Chicago Mercantile Exchange where his friend Leo Melamed wanted to develop an unregulated market in foreign currencies, played a significant role in urging financial liberalisation and licence for the trading of new instruments. Friedman argued that asset instability would converge to a stable equilibrium and reiterated the 1890s argument that financial derivatives are a useful protection again financial instability. When the world moved into a phase of greater economic and financial instability, monetarists reassured everyone that all was for the best and urged monetary policy to eliminate the instability of prices. The resulting monetary policy activism destabilised interest rates. To stock options and exchange rate futures were added interest rate futures.

In the 1980s and 1990s, financial innovations continued apace with new instruments tied to the values of stock portfolios, or converting one type of debt instrument (say bank loans) into collateralised debt obligation, a process known as securitisation. When the instability started affecting banks themselves, new credit insurance instruments, latterly credit default swaps, emerged. The prospectus for all these innovations expressed their function as 'risk management', i.e., the elimination of instability of asset values. But as we now know these innovations were just devices for transferring such risks around the market rather than eliminating them. The more that derivatives were used to pass potential losses onto someone else, the more of everyone else's risks everyone took on.

It is even possible, in this situation, to characterise a peculiar property of financial innovation that involves transfer of liability for a loss through a variety of financial instruments until it can be placed in an instrument that the buyer does not understand. At this point, the incomprehension of the buyer, his apparent contentment with holding a liability that he does not know he has, and the satisfaction of the seller in transferring a liability to someone who is transferring again, eliminate the market incentive for any further innovation. Perhaps a fourth kind of financial innovation emerges in which the liabilities that everyone who operates in banking and the financial markets takes on are transformed into liabilities that are unknown. In markets driven by perceived risk, such as the markets for financial derivatives, innovation turns known risks into unknown ones. This makes us all contented because what the heart (or the accountant) doesn't know, it (or that accountant) cannot grieve over. Marking to market, or valuing instruments in accounts according to their market value, embeds collective ignorance in balance sheets. There it rests until history uncovers the true value of all liabilities.

Not all financial innovation is a response to credit expansion and asset instability. Some innovations have been genuinely useful where they have facilitated payments and access to credit, for example credit cards, or the single European currency (a government, rather than a commercial bank venture). However, the driving force for most recent financial innovations is not any actual need outside the financial markets or the convenience of the public, but the instability of asset markets as monetary innovation extends and credit adds ephemeral liquidity to markets. There is little even financial need for most of these innovations, since financial risks are most conveniently and cheaply hedged by holding liquid assets or government bonds, what Keynes called liquidity preference. The reason why financial derivatives have proliferated is because financial intermediaries are using them to profit from financial instability (rather than just to eliminate the risks attendant upon that instability), or are obtaining fee income from selling such instruments to their customers.

Following the recent financial crisis with the spreading reduction in credit (so-called deleveraging) as debts are repaid, it is likely financial innovation will cease to offer novelty in the financial markets. The resumption of financial innovation in the future obviously depends on the regulation that emerges from the present crisis. Some of those markets are now returning to a 1940s-style phase of increasing Government controls, and absorbing rapid increases in Government debt. There is also an increased reluctance among the wealthy and their fund managers to hold innovative financial assets. But, more importantly, if less visibly, the pace of such innovation also depends on the stability of asset markets in the future and how the distribution of wealth evolves. If the inevitable financial reconstruction results in more stable markets, and social and fiscal policy removes concentrations of wealth that require active markets for their liquidity, then financial innovation will mostly wither, and the resources tied up in it can be applied to more socially useful activities.

5

The Inflation of Goodwill

Goodwill is a politely mendacious courtesy which accountancy pays to the financial markets. Such amiable fictions populate financial economics in which the function of financial markets, to facilitate sale and purchase of financial assets, is ennobled by an ability to determine the true value of those assets. Because the prices in financial assets rarely express the true value of anything, a dignified name that confirms the correctness of the market's judgement must be given to the deviation of market value from the assets represented by that market value. Goodwill is one such dignified expression.

Goodwill is the value placed on the expectation that the clients or customers of an established company will continue to patronise it out of habit or confidence in the conduct of its business. In practice, it is today simply the amount by which the price of a going concern exceeds the sum of fair values of all of its other net assets. In other words, it is the amount of money that may be paid to the owners of a business over and above the costs of merely buying the assets that the company use. When financial markets are inflated, the scope for goodwill is correspondingly expanded.

The origin of the term lies in changes in accounting practice that accompanied the rise of the capital market in the second half of the nineteenth century. The easing of the establishment of joint stock companies during this period facilitated the purchase of many retail businesses, whose previous owners were paid for referring their customers to the business under new management or ownership. However, today goodwill is used to pay the existing owners of a company's equity a price for their stock that may be inflated above the value of any actual underlying assets by the more active capital markets of the late twentieth century. It has nothing to do with any reference that previous owners of a business may give to its existing customers because the owners of the most significant companies (i.e., the largest companies) today are institutional investors, pension funds, insurance companies and mutual funds. They never, in the normal course of their business, address the customers of the businesses that they own.

Goodwill purchased in this way has wider implications because the cost of it is treated as a business expense. In the United States and Canada this expense is amortized against company earnings over a period of up to forty years. After a company has been purchased, these amortization payments are purely book-keeping transactions. It has therefore been argued that the recording of these payments in the income and expenditure statement of a company makes that statement less clearly a reflection of actual business income and expenditure. In the UK an accounting standard in force since 1984 recommends that goodwill should 'normally' be written off immediately after acquisition against the owners' equity or reserves. However, such immediate write-off this can lead to extreme shifts in the 'leverage' or gearing of a company (the ratio of its debt to equity).[1] It is not unknown for such a write-off to result in negative owners' equity. Even before that arises, the sudden fall in the value of owners' equity may cause difficulty where a company has loan agreements that stipulate a maximum permissible leverage ratio. Such shifts in the value of owners' equity also affect the vulnerability of a company to takeover, or even to reporting, as the London Stock Exchange obliges its companies to do, where the payment for a company represents 15 per cent or more of the acquiring company's equity.

Because business expenses reduce the tax liability of companies, the accounting treatment of goodwill, that is, whether and how it is amortized, may have significant tax implications for a company. Among service companies with limited scope for capital investments that may be set against tax over a period of years, goodwill may be an important factor in the tax planning of a company.

The significance of goodwill in corporate finance has been inflated by the proliferation of mergers and takeovers in active capital markets. The emergence of such markets in Europe and other parts of the world extends the geographical area where goodwill has fiscal and accounting importance.

Merger and takeover activity today has less to do with creating more efficient business organisations and more to do with generating cash flow from the inflation of the capital markets, i.e., buying a financial asset in the expectation of selling it at a higher price in the future. Goodwill must be paid generously to the existing owners of a firm in the expectation that in the future such goodwill will be rewarded with an even greater generosity at the markets rise. This kind of goodwill was noted in the early part of the twentieth century in the Industrial Commission hearings of the United States Congress, whose testimonies were pored over by Thorstein Veblen. His *Theory of Business Enterprise*, published in 1906, is an essential source on the use of goodwill to create fictitious values for financial assets.

6

Leverage and Balance Sheet Inflation

The terms 'leverage' (or its UK equivalent 'gearing') and 'deleveraging' have acquired renewed currency with the crisis that broke out in 2007. Leverage is the indebtedness of a company, or the process of increasing the indebtedness of a company (as in the phrase 'highly leveraged company' or 'acquiring leverage'). It is usually measured by one of two 'gearing' ratios. Capital or financial gearing is the amount of debt that a company has relative to its total capital. Alternatively, income gearing is the ratio of a company's debt to its total income.

Until the twentieth century, income gearing was the common measure of leverage. This reflected a corporate practice in which the only possible gainful use of debt, that is, aside from its traditional unproductive use in financing consumption or government, was to finance commerce or industry. It followed that the key indicator in determining the amount of borrowing was the possible income that it might generate in trade or production.

With the emergence of active markets in corporate finance, towards the end of the nineteenth century in Britain and the United States, the scope for the gainful employment of leverage extended beyond commerce and industry, and into the capital market itself. Once that market became sufficiently large, the return from profitable trade in it was determined by the total amount of capital that could be turned over in that market. In these circumstances, the major consideration was no longer potential future income in trade or production because these are irrelevant in determining income from arbitraging in the capital market, but the amount of capital that could be applied to a profitable arbitrage. That amount of capital, and hence the income from it, was maximised by adding borrowing to equity.

From this emerged the measure of leverage common today, namely the ratio of debt to total capital.

The roots of this change in definition, in the changing business of finance, was obscured in the 1950s by the famous Miller-Modigliani Theorem, which claimed to prove that the true value of a corporation is not affected by the division of its capital into equity and debt. But this is under the assumption of a perfect capital market after all arbitrage possibilities have been exhausted, so that the return on debt was ultimately provided by income from commerce or industry rather than further financial transactions. The 'Theorem' set off a number of hares in the academic finance literature to determine whether variations in leverage were caused by capital market imperfections, or differences in the tax treatment of interest on debt, as opposed to the tax liability on the return to equity (see essay 9).

Today it is increasingly recognised that the business opportunities available to a company, and its liquidity are clearly affected by its leverage. A company with $1 million of equity, tied up in productive equipment and work in progress, is a relatively illiquid company that may experience financial difficulties if a larger than expected bill needs to be paid. That same company with an additional $10 million of debt invested in the money market is a highly liquid company that can cope with larger than expected payments. It can undertake new projects without having to waste management time in finding financial backers. Most importantly of all, it can engage in speculative buying and selling of companies in the capital market without reducing its liquidity as long as that market stays liquid.[1] With the expansion of capital market financing beyond the United States and United Kingdom into Europe and emerging markets elsewhere, leverage is becoming an increasingly widely used way of making medium-sized businesses into large corporations without the tedium of expanding productive or commercial capacity.

Leverage can be managed without adverse financial consequences for firms as long as they hold sufficient quantities of short-term or liquid financial assets against longer borrowing. However, if financial markets suddenly become illiquid (i.e., with very little buying in them) as has happened in the recent financial crisis, a firm may find itself without sufficient liquid assets to manage that gearing. In this situation, firms try to 'deleverage', i.e., reduce their debt. Where firms reduce debt by cutting back on their usual (non-financial) business expenditures, this creates the process of debt-deflation that Irving Fisher believed was the essence of economic depression.[2]

Deleveraging is not just a process of debt repayment. It involves cancelling both bank credit and loans (or reducing the amount of loan securities in circulation). In this way, the balance sheet of the financial system is reduced. But this is only part of the process. When debts are repaid, money that firms have thrown into circulation in the course of production and exchange fails to come back to them in the form of sales revenue, because firms, households or governments have preferred to use the income obtained from firms' expenditure on repaying debt. Deleveraging therefore inflicts losses on firms. This is the main mechanism spreading economic crisis through the economy.

7

Inflation in Financial Markets

At the heart of financial instability and crisis are processes of inflation and deflation in credit or financial markets. This is one of the least understood aspects of finance, and it is usually wholly ignored in financial economics. Yet it is impossible to understand the seemingly permanent state of fluctuation in financial markets, or to conduct monetary policy effectively, without some insight into these processes.

Financial inflation is best described as the rise in the value of the financial sector of the economy (banking and finance) in relation to the value of the rest of the economy. For example, at the end of the twentieth century, the value of all financial assets in the United States was equal to more than three times the Gross National Product of the United States. In the middle of that century, the value of all financial assets in the US was around double that country's GNP. Since Gross National Product is a flow, and the value of financial assets is a stock, we should, strictly speaking, compare the value of financial assets against the value of some other assets (for example, the capital stock of the economy). But there are problems with measuring such stocks accurately. Financial inflation may nevertheless be observed when credit expands more rapidly than output, or when prices of financial securities rise more rapidly that prices of real output (consumption or investment goods) or wages.

Financial inflation becomes embedded in capitalism when commodity production (the production of goods and services for exchange, rather than for immediate consumption) comes to be mediated by credit, rather than commodity money, such as gold. It is possible for an economy to experience an inflation of commodity money. Such was the case, notoriously, in Spain after the discovery of America when large quantities of gold were shipped from Mexico to Spain. These shipments caused a huge increase in prices, as noted by David Hume, who inferred from it his Quantity Theory of Money (the view that prices change in proportion to changes in the stock of money). But they did not inflate financial markets because there were no proper financial markets. Gold was borrowed and lent in eighteenth century Spain, and much of it was hoarded (i.e., take out of circulation and kept safe for future spending). The Spanish banking system (unlike the English one, see below) did not expand beyond the credit needs of trade.

The modern capitalist economy uses credit rather than commodity money. Credit is simply a bank deposit or a loan from a bank, which may be used to make payments, as savings, or to buy financial securities. Credit will expand faster than output as intermediation is extended, i.e., as more payments are made using balances at a financial intermediary (usually a bank) as means of payment for goods and services in the real economy.[1] Strictly speaking this is not financial inflation but simply a shift in the kind of medium of exchange that an economy uses. From using cash (banknotes and coins) as means of payment, the economy now uses credit as the common means of payment. This is apparent as economies move from being rural economies with industrial enclaves, or semi-industrialised economies, into being urban economies with a rural fringe. Examples of semi-industrialised economies in the process of becoming fully financially intermediated urban economies are the countries of Eastern Europe, Greece, Ireland, Portugal, Mexico, Brazil and Argentina.

In contrast to wider use of credit in the real economy, financial inflation occurs when credit is expanded and taken up in a more rapid turnover in the financial markets and the price of financial assets. Some financial inflation inevitably occurs as credit is more widely used in the economy, and the classical political economists following Ricardo believed that some financial inflation (in the form of deposits placed in banks) is necessary for credit creation. The banks that keep credit accounts need to organise markets among themselves to be able to trade credit instruments, such as bills of exchange and bonds, and to be able to buy and sell central bank credit (known as Federal Funds in the United States) which gives them access to notes and coins issued by the central bank. As more credit is used in the economy, so the activity of these markets becomes more sophisticated and turnover in them rises.

The discount market in the United Kingdom is a good example of the financial inflation that accompanies wider use of credit. The turnover of this discount market (trading short-term government and company bills) is 12 or 13 times the Gross National Product of the United Kingdom! Further financial inflation occurs as markets for longer-term securities (i.e., stock markets) become active. This becomes an issue for economists. Some of them, such as Patinkin or McKinnon and Shaw, argue that financial inflation merely shows how sophisticated and modern an economy is becoming. Others argue that it distorts economic activity and leads to speculative booms and subsequent economic crises.

Financial inflation is not a problem in the general equilibrium models widely used to analyse finance in the economy. It is usually treated, for example in the theory of Léon Walras or Tobin's 'q' model, as an increase in saving which will push down the rate of interest (or the cost of financing investment) and thereby elicit a corresponding increase in investment. However, this is only an equilibrium that is supposed to be reached *after* all the effects of the financial inflation have worked themselves out. Many economists argue that financial inflation does not lead to such an equilibrium, but that it distorts economic activity and makes the economy more unstable.

History

The first modern financial inflation occurred at the end of the seventeenth century, as a direct result of the inflow of Spanish gold and its transformation of the London financial markets. Reporting the research of Earl J. Hamilton, and W. R. Scott, Keynes noted the significance of financial inflation for the establishment of financial markets in these terms:

> The expedition of Mr. Phipps (afterwards Sir W. Phipps) to recover a Spanish treasure ship which was believed to have sunk some fifty years before off the coast of Hispaniola, is one of the most extraordinary records of improbable success. He returned to London in 1688, having fished out of the sea a sum estimated at between £250,000 and £300,000 and paid a dividend to his shareholders of 10,000 per cent (even Drake had only distributed a dividend of 4,700 per cent). The excitement and the stimulus occasioned by this event was the proximate cause of the remarkable stock exchange boom which reached its climax in 1692–5 and ended with the foundation of the Bank of England, a stock exchange

list (with 137 securities quoted) on modern lines, and the reform of the currency by Locke and Newton ...[2]

However, this inflation was followed by the Mississippi and South Sea Bubbles of 1710–1720. There are obvious similarities between these events and later financial inflations, with credit being extended to enable speculators to buy the shares (commons stocks) issued by the companies. This inflow of credit into the stocks markets pushed share prices to dizzying heights. Fortunes were made by those lucky enough to buy and then sell in time. When the inflow of credit faltered, the inflation collapsed. Credit disappeared until the markets stabilised again.

For over a hundred years after the South Sea and Mississippi Bubbles, economists were very wary of allowing banks and credit institutions to develop. In contrast to his otherwise *laisser-faire* views, Adam Smith (1723–1790), for example, argued that banks need to be strictly controlled to make sure that they did not issue more credit than was strictly required for trade. (This was known as the Real Bills Doctrine.) David Ricardo (1772–1823) and John Stuart Mill (1806–1873) argued that paper money issued by banks needed to be strictly controlled otherwise it would lead to general price inflation, as well as financial inflation. In spite of this, the nineteenth century was punctuated by speculative and financial crises, which were usually attributed to financial inflation, such as an excess of bank credit.

In the 1860s, in order to facilitate the expansion of business finance, Companies' Acts were passed in Britain and in the United States. By the 1880s and the 1890s, there was sufficient financial instability in the capital and banking markets for the American economist Thorstein Veblen (1857–1929) to develop a theory of financial inflation leading to crisis in his book *The Theory of Business Enterprise*. Following the 1929 Wall Street Crash and the subsequent Great Depression of the 1930s, the most distinguished economists Ralph Hawtrey (1879–1971)[3], John Maynard Keynes (1883–1946)[4], Irving Fisher (1867–1947)[5] and Friedrich von Hayek (1899–1992)[6], who otherwise could not agree with each other on the nature of capitalism and its instabilities, all believed that financial inflation had caused the over-investment which they supposed was the cause of the depression. Thereafter they all developed widely differing ideas about how capitalism could be made stable. But around 1930–1931 they were all in agreement that the financial inflation of the 1920s in America had caused the depression. As a consequence, there was broad agreement during the 1930s when the United States Congress passed legislation to control banks and finance more strictly.

After the Second World War, financial systems were stabilised by the 1944 Bretton Woods Agreement and the financial and capital controls that supported it. However, in the post-War period, the United States experienced a major outflow of dollars, in large part because of chronic balance of payments' deficits. These dollars accumulated in the unregulated 'off-shore' markets known as the Euro-dollar markets. As the Euro-dollar market expanded, and with it smaller markets for other currencies held outside their countries of issue, it became more and more difficult to maintain the system of fixed exchange rates and capital controls. The fixed exchange rate system collapsed in 1971 and was followed by the removal of controls on capital exports by the US, by the UK in 1979, and by the countries in the European Union in 1990–1991. The last decades of the twentieth century were marked by financial crises, the 1982 Third World Debt Crisis, the 1995 Mexican crisis, the East Asian Crisis of 1997, the Russian Crisis of 1998 and so on. The global capitalist economy that followed the collapse of the Soviet Union in 1991 has turned out to be remarkably unstable. Financial economists, such as Hyman P. Minsky and Charles P. Kindleberger, have argued that this instability is due to financial inflation.

Bank Inflation

From the 1920s onwards, with the work of Wicksell, Hawtrey and Hayek[7], it was thought that lowering the rate of interest below a 'natural' rate of interest (at which saving and investment were supposed to be equal) would cause a credit inflation. The lower 'market' rate of interest was supposed to induce entrepreneurs to increase their investment with borrowed money. This was believed to cause a disequilibrium in which investment is higher than 'voluntary saving'. However, the extra investment would generate extra revenue in the investment goods sector of the economy and subsequently extra spending on consumer goods. This would be inflationary (because of investment being in excess of 'voluntary' saving). As prices and production rose, profits would rise too. The additional profits were called by Hayek 'forced' savings which then balanced the additional investment. Finally, when the new productive capacity came into production, entrepreneurs would realise that they had been induced into making excessive investments. The excess capacity would cause investment to fall. Alternatively, the monetary authorities would increase the market rate of interest to reduce the credit expansion, and investment would fall off, leaving excess capacity and lower profits.

However, this analysis, essentially that put forward by Hayek and Wicksell, does not explain what happens to bank balance sheets when credit expands. Already in the nineteenth century, among the Banking School, the Principle of Reflux (or the Credit Multiplier) was known. This is the principle that bank loans re-appear in the banking system as deposits. It works as follows. Suppose National Bank lends to entrepreneur Martinez $100,000 to buy machinery for his factory. Martinez will use the credit to pay entrepreneur Lopez for machinery that Lopez manufactures. Lopez will now pay $100,000 into his account at Capital Bank. Capital Bank now has an additional $100,000 which it can loan out to its customers, even if Lopez is only repaying a loan which he had taken out to pay for manufacturing his machinery.

In the nineteenth century, the possibility of credit being multiplied in this way was thought to be a potent way of raising prices in the economy because the 'supply of money' was increasing as credit expanded. Until recently, there was thought to be only one limitation on such credit expansion: the requirement that banks have to have sufficient notes and coins in their tills to enable their depositors (and those who borrow from them) to make withdrawals in cash. If a bank ran out of notes and coins, then it would collapse. Under the Gold Standard that regulated money and international payments before the First World War, the amount of notes and coins in issue was supposed to be limited by the amount of gold reserves in the central bank. If there was not enough gold in those reserves, the central bank could raise the rate of interest paid on gold deposits. In many developing countries, dollars and convertible currencies now play the part of gold reserves for their central banks. If the rate of interest on reserve deposits was not enough to bring in sufficient gold (or foreign currency reserves) from abroad, then the central bank was obliged to reduce the amount of notes and coins in circulation. If a bank ran out of notes and coins, then it collapsed, unless the central bank was allowed to issue extra cash, or borrow gold or foreign currency. In advanced capitalist countries today, the widespread use of credit to make payments (by cheques, transferring deposits from one account to another) means that in practice only a minor part of credit balances is ever withdrawn as cash.

Since 1971, no major trading country has tied its currency to gold. There is therefore no limitation on the amount of credit expansion that can take place, even though banks are supposed to keep some proportion of their deposits in accounts at the central bank, which can then be used to draw notes and coins from the central bank. Post-Keynesian economists such as Nicholas Kaldor and Victoria Chick have argued that banks can always 'buy' reserves, in the inter-bank market in Britain or the Federal Funds market in the United States, to give themselves sufficient cash against any amount of lending or deposit creation.[8] The possibility of indefinite credit expansion suggests that there can be much greater price inflation in the economy, as well as the kind of economic instability that Hayek, Hawtrey and Wicksell analysed.

Financial Inflation in Securities Markets

Bank inflation is supposed to destabilise the economy by raising prices of goods and services and eventually wages if the additional credit is used to by extra goods (investment goods or stocks of finished products for sale) or if it is used to buy assets that are inelastic in supply (land, buildings). In the latter case in particular, a speculative 'bubble' may emerge in which asset prices rise until demand for the asset falls away. If the asset was bought using credit, then an eventual fall in the price of the asset reduces the value of the security or collateral against which money has been borrowed. If the value of the asset falls below the amount of the loan, then the borrower is technically insolvent. If the loan has to be repaid from the market price obtained for the asset on sale, then there will not be enough from the sales proceeds to repay the loan. In this way, borrowers can be forced into bankruptcy.

In more sophisticated financial systems, there are markets for securities ('valuable paper' or financial assets), ranging from short-term bills sold at a discount by governments and companies and then repaid in full after, say, thirty days, to long-term government bonds and stocks and shares. Government bonds in particular are held by banks as risk-free assets. Financial speculators make money by borrowing money to buy financial assets whose value is expected to increase in value by an amount more than the costs of borrowing. These financial assets can be stocks or shares, or foreign currency that is appreciating. Such speculators are known as 'bulls'. (More infrequently, 'bears' try to make money by 'shorting' markets, i.e., selling assets that they do not own with delayed delivery in the hope that, when the time comes to deliver, they will be able to buy the asset for delivery at a lower price.) In this way, a financial inflation may appear to have little effect on the 'real' economy (i.e., prices, wages and output outside the financial markets) while the inflation is taking place.

From the 1970s onwards, Charles P. Kindleberger and Hyman P. Minsky have argued that this kind of financial inflation is nevertheless dangerous because the eventual 'disinflation' causes the financial markets to collapse with unfortunate consequences for non-financial businesses that rely on them for finance. The main evidence for this has been the history of past financial inflations and collapses, in particular the 1929 Crash and the Depression which followed it. For Charles Kindleberger, the mainsprings of financial inflations are essentially psychological: people cannot resist opportunities to make large amounts of money through speculation. Any economic event, technological breakthrough or change in economic circumstances causes wealthy individuals to re-assess the future value their assets. If they expect those assets to increase in value by more than a certain proportion, they will buy more of those assets. The increased demand for them causes their prices to rise, as predicted by their initial purchasers. The capital gains made by them attract more buyers. In this way, an asset boom develops. As demand for the asset increases, it becomes more difficult to buy, because existing owners hold on to their assets to make the largest possible gain on them. The boom now turns into a mania, providing that wealthy individuals have enough liquidity or access to credit to keep buying.[9]

At this point, according to Kindleberger, people are so desperate to make their fortune out of the rising asset values that it is easy to deceive them. Fraud emerges on the fringes of legitimate financial dealings. When the fraud is revealed, and when investors run out of money to buy any more of the asset, the 'bubble' bursts. When the price of the asset stops rising, holders of the asset discover that they must sell quickly if they are to realise their profits. But with the price of the asset now no longer rising, the number of investors wishing to buy is reduced. The pressure of selling intentions pushes down the price of the asset. Holders of the asset are now under even more pressure to sell to avoid or minimise losses. The initial selling turns into panic selling. Capital gains are wiped out. Those who borrowed in order to buy the asset are left with debts exceeding the value of their assets. If they cannot pay their debts, they are ruined.

Capital gains and investors' expectations play a crucial role in Kindleberger's analysis of financial inflation. The origins of this kind of analysis lie in Keynes's *General Theory of Employment, Interest and Money*. In chapter 12 of that book on 'The State of Long-Term Expectation', Keynes put forward the idea that the true value of financial assets cannot be known because the future stream of income from them, which is discounted to arrive at their present value, cannot be ascertained. Therefore, the prices of financial securities are set by the markets according to whatever traders in them subjectively believe is a correct price. This conventional valuation of assets can vary from day to day. The day to day variation in this valuation is the basis of capital gains or losses. Keynes then argued that increasingly in financial markets traders buy financial assets for capital gains because this provides them with a more immediate profit than waiting for future income, in the form of interest or dividends, to come in. He called such investment for capital gains 'speculation' and distinguished it from 'enterprise' by which he meant investment for future income. He argued that enterprise was productive, while speculation was unproductive.

In one of his final chapters in the *General Theory*, chapter 22, 'Notes on the Trade Cycle', Keynes used similar ideas to explain the business cycle. Essentially, he argued that business investment, which is the main factor in capitalist business cycles, tends to fluctuate because businessmen who make investment decisions are sometimes more optimistic and have more confidence about investing for future income, and sometimes are pessimistic and view the prospects of future profit income with less confidence.[10]

During the 1970s, Hyman P. Minsky took up these ideas and developed them into a theory of the business cycle in which financial inflation plays a major part. His major innovation was to combine the theory of investment of the Polish economist Michał Kalecki with his own original theory of financing structures. At its simplest, Kalecki's theory of investment argues that, because wages are by and large spent on consumption goods and profits are by and large saved, the more capitalists spend on investment, the more profits they themselves will receive over and above the wages they pay out to their workers. However, rising investment (and rising profits) eventually create such a large capital stock that excess capacity induces a fall in investment, and hence profits. The fall in investment turns the boom into a recession.[11]

Minsky argued that all investment, indeed, all financial market transactions, involve the creation of future payment commitments and future income.[12] These he called financing structures which have to be settled out of income streams or new financing. Therefore a major consequence of financial inflation is an increase in future payment obligations against future income secured that is expected from such inflation. Minsky put forward three types of financing structures. There is first of all 'hedge' finance where the commitment to pay in the future is matched by an equal income stream that some other economic unit is obliged to pay. An example of this is the obligation of banks to pay a 'floating' rate of interest to depositors, matched by a 'floating' rate which the bank charges to its borrowers. This is the safest kind of financing structure.

'Speculative' financing involves entering into payments commitments which may or may not be matched and therefore carry some element of financial risk. For example, a fixed rate loan by a bank carries the risk that the rate of interest which the bank pays on its deposits may rise above the interest that it receives on this asset. This financial deficit would then have to be financed out of previous saving or by new financing. Finally, 'Ponzi' financing consists of issuing additional future financial commitments in order to pay for current commitments. The classic example of this is so-called 'pyramid' banking, where high returns are paid for deposits out of new deposits, whose returns then have to be paid out of even larger future deposits. (Charles Ponzi, after whom Minsky named this kind of financing, swindled investors in Boston with a pyramid banking scheme between 1919 and 1921.)

Minsky argued that during an economic boom, the financing of investment loads up the non-financial business sector with financial liabilities. As the payments due on these financial liabilities increase, the cash flow to pay them from the operating profits of industrial and commercial activities is taken up increasingly with the costs of financing. When investment is reduced, so too are profits and the cash flow to pay financing costs. When the cash flow is insufficient to pay these costs, companies can carry on for a while by raising additional finance to pay current financing costs. But this is Ponzi finance which eventually leads to insupportable financial costs and financial crisis. Minsky linked this analysis with Keynes by saying that a period of 'tranquillity', marked by stable profits, encourages the expectation of stable profits in the future. Additional speculative financing then takes place. When this proves unsustainable, Ponzi financing is increasingly used to maintain commercial operations. Finally, assets are sold causing a collapse in asset prices that have been inflated by the boom. Thus economic booms are marked by a build-up of debt (financial inflation) and the progressive addition of speculative and Ponzi financing in the economy.[13]

Both Kindleberger and Minsky lay great store by the effectiveness of lender of last resort facilities in the economy. Since the nineteenth century, central banks have emerged as lenders of last resort to banks within their jurisdictions. If commercial banks run out of cash to pay their liabilities (usually withdrawals of deposits or repayments of borrowing), the financial authorities will, if they wish the failing bank to survive, lend to them or organise loans for them from other institutions. Traditionally this is done at a higher rate of interest than that prevailing in the market to discourage excessive use of such assistance. For Kindleberger and Minsky, lender of last resort facilities allow the refinancing of economic units with financial deficits (negative cash flows), enabling a more orderly reorganisation and reduction of financial liabilities, i.e., a financial deflation without financial collapse. Nowadays, at the end of the twentieth century, such lender of last resort finance is frequently offered in the form of new capital (shares or common stock) which enables the failing financial institution to pay its liabilities. It also gives the institution putting in the new capital, the central bank or the Government Treasury, control over the failing institution, a claim on any profits which the failing institution may make in the future, or the possibility of selling its controlling interest in the institution at a profit in the future.

Minsky was also an advocate of using monetary policy to reduce the rate of interest in times of financial inflation. He argued that because the cash outflow commitments of borrowers are linked to the rate of interest, lower rates of interest reduce those cash outflows. In this way, financing structures can be made more compatible with income receipts: Ponzi financing structures become more speculative, and speculative financing structures become more hedged. However, the rehabilitation of financing structures in this way is a way of making bad debt better, or even good debt. It does not deal with the problem that financial inflation results in too much debt, whether good or bad. As early as 1933, Irving Fisher had argued in his famous paper *The Debt Deflation Theory of Great Depressions* that the Great Depression was caused by excessive debt absorbing too high a proportion of corporate income.[14] As the Third World Debt Crisis showed in the last two decades of the twentieth century, the refinancing, even on improved terms, of excessive debt may make such debt more manageable. But it can still leave economic units unable to engage in the kind of major capital expenditures that are required to get an economy out of a depression. In his paper, Fisher makes the intriguing suggestion, later taken up by Minsky, that a credit economy is characterised by two sets of prices. One is for goods, services and labour, and determines relative incomes in the real economy. The other is the set of prices in the financial markets, both asset prices and rates of return in the future. Fisher argued that the burden of debt depends on how these sets of prices change relative to each other. If financial inflation proceeds at a rate faster than general price inflation, then debt deflation squeezes expenditure in the economy. If general price inflation proceeds more rapidly than financial inflation, then firms' income rises more rapidly than their financing costs, and they can extend their expenditure on production and capital works.

The Theory of Capital Market Inflation

It has already been mentioned that one of the few times when economists with widely differing views on the nature and future of the capitalist economy agreed occurred in 1930, when virtually all economists believed that the stock market boom of the 1920s had led to over-investment. Towards the end of the twentieth century, as stock markets around the world boomed without inducing major investment in fixed capital except in some highly speculative areas of electronics and information technology, it was equally commonly agreed that the main effect of financial inflation in the stock market was a *wealth effect* on consumption. Essentially, the higher the stock market, the higher the household consumption of those owning financial assets. This wealth effect had already been noted by Keynes in his *Treatise on Money* in 1930. However, a more sophisticated view of how a stock market inflation affects the economy is presented by the theory of capital market inflation.[15]

The theory of capital market inflation is a non-equilibrium theory of capital markets. It argues that the actual value of the capital market, by which is meant the market for long-term securities, is determined by the inflow of funds into that market. Most of that inflow is then taken out by issues of securities (bonds) by governments, and a large part of the remainder of the inflow is taken out by securities issued by corporations. The balance is a net excess inflow which forms the liquidity of the market, circulating around in it until it is 'taken out' by an additional stock issue. The net excess inflow therefore determines the value of turnover in stocks and the liquidity of the market. It provides the margin of liquidity in the market that allows it to absorb a modest degree of net sales by financial investors. Stock markets therefore crash not because they are out of equilibrium, but because their disequilibrium has been insufficient to accumulate enough excess net inflows to accommodate the currently desired net sales by financial investors.

The net excess inflow into the capital market determines stock prices: when this inflow increases, brokers faced with rising purchase orders raise prices to induce stockholders to sell and maintain brokers' stock balances. In this situation, turnover and prices rise in the market. Extended over a longer period of time, a growing net excess inflow gives rise to a process of capital market inflation. However, not all stock prices rise equally or proportionately. Loan stocks (bonds or debentures) with a maturity date on which they are repaid have the value of the stocks on that maturity date fixed by the terms on which the stocks were issued. Usually this is printed on the stock certificate as the nominal value of the stock and the amount that its holder will obtain when the stock is repaid. This clearly indicates to financial investors an eventual value of the stock which cannot be exceeded on that maturity date. With longer-term stocks, capital market inflation may drive their prices above their repayment or nominal value before they mature. But this 'trading above par' would only be temporary until repayment. Irredeemable stocks, such as equities (common stocks), do not have any fixed nominal value in the future. Capital gains in these stocks are therefore most likely to be sustained and further increased. A process of capital market inflation therefore increases disproportionately the market values of the longer term and irredeemable stocks.

Capital market inflation has economy-wide consequences because of the way in which it changes the behaviour of all those affected by it. In the first place, it whets the appetite of financial investors for longer-term stocks on which a capital gain may be made, in addition to revenue from dividends and interest. In this way, it reduces the liquidity preference of financial investors precisely when the additional money that has caused the inflation is flowing into the market and when an *increase* in liquidity preference would be necessary to maintain 'equilibrium' in the capital market. Thus capital market inflation is not only a phenomenon created by disequilibrium. It is also itself profoundly disequilibrating.

For stock-issuing corporations and governments, the increased demand for long-term stocks is a blessing that is only mildly off-set by the dangers of over-capitalisation. Corporations find that they can issue equity at lower earnings per share than previously and at a lower cost because their stockholders now obtain and expect capital gains, paid by other financial investors in the future rather than by the corporations. Indeed, since pre-tax profits are calculated by deducting interest payments from operating profits, an easy way of making pre-tax profits levitate is by issuing equity and using the proceeds to retire debt. When all the possibilities of such retirement have been exhausted in a given corporation, profits may be further levitated by taking over (acquiring) or merging with another indebted corporation. When the possibilities of acquisition have been exhausted, subsidiaries may be 'deglomerated' and brought to market with new share issues. Above all, in a period of capital market inflation, companies with access to the capital market find that they can become large not through so-called 'organic' growth, building more and more factories and offering more and more goods and services to their customers. Organic growth of this kind involves too much financial risk in tying up capital for too long in relatively illiquid plant, machinery and real estate. It is much easier to issue excess capital and use that capital to buy financial assets which, under financial inflation, are more easily resold at a profit than factories and shops. In this way, far from encouraging greater fixed capital investment, as Hawtrey, Hayek and Keynes (before the *General Theory*) had thought, capital market inflation causes companies to turn from productive to financial activities and become rentiers in their own right. Recent studies have shown that the holdings of liquid assets by US corporations have risen during the final decades of the twentieth century. This does not mean that these corporations are in a sound financial state with large liquid reserves. It simply means that they are becoming financial intermediaries, and their liquid assets are their security against their excessive capital. Because of that, companies have to be even more careful about investing in relatively illiquid fixed capital or technology, and, if they do so, such investment is more speculative because of the larger financial liabilities of companies.

In an era of capital market inflation, the productive activities of the modern corporation are therefore incidental to the restructuring of corporate balance sheets and the making of money by buying and selling subsidiaries. In this way, from being a facility in which corporations may regulate their liquidity by refinancing internally-financed fixed capital investments, the capital market comes to absorb the liquidity of corporations. During the 1990s many US corporations used their reserves to buy back their shares in order to keep up their prices. Towards the end of the decade, when prices in stock markets stopped rising, many corporations even borrowed money to buy in their stocks. Minsky would have called this Ponzi finance, because the borrowing is not used to generate income with which to pay for the borrowing. Capital market inflation thus ruptures any connection between the market prices of stocks and any presumed or expected earnings or profits from any underlying productive capital assets.

For governments, capital market inflation offers new financing opportunities. Capital markets have traditionally taken a hostile attitude towards deficit financing because of the perceived reduction in the scarcity value of government debt that it entails. However, for governments which have inherited substantial commercial public sector companies, the development of privatisation since the 1980s offers a form of deficit financing which does not reduce the scarcity value of government stocks. This is because privatisation is a way of financing current government expenditure by issuing stocks which are the liabilities not of the government but of the companies privatised. While it has been publicised as an exciting, free-enterprise-supporting financial innovation, it was in fact pioneered by John Law with the Mississippi and South Sea Companies in the early part of the eighteenth century.

With households enjoying the benefits of unprecedented capital gains through household direct ownership of stocks and their indirect ownership through pension, insurance and mutual funds, the only losers in the process are the banks. As noted above, capital market inflation induces the issue of long-term stocks and equity by governments and large corporations to replace debt. This is to the disadvantage of banks because governments and large corporations have traditionally been the best and safest borrowers from banks. The capital market inflation dating from roughly the mid-1970s has therefore been characterised by a process of bank disintermediation. With the loss of their best borrowers, banks have been forced to develop their lending to more marginal borrowers carrying greater risks: syndicated lending to developing countries, followed by heavy advances against property (real estate) and latterly financial futures, were accompanied by increased lending to less liquid borrowers in the form of consumer credit and loans to smaller companies.

This is not necessarily apparent from an examination of bank balance sheets. These show additional liquidity secured by access to larger money markets in which the big corporations are now lending out their liquidity and by innovations such as securitization. This last enables banks to sell the stronger portions of their loan book as bonds into an inflated capital market. Lending to governments and large corporations still figures in the balance sheets. However, this is not direct lending, but the purchase of government bills and commercial paper in the money markets at rates of discount that offer little or no margin over the banks' own cost of capital. The outcome is that state of incipient financial crisis in the banking system, occasionally breaking into financial distress and collapse, which Minsky identified with financial fragility.

In the advanced capitalist countries, capital market inflation has been induced by a structural factor and a political-economic one. The structural factor has been the history of chronic balance of payments deficits in the United States. Moreover, since 1944 the international monetary system has, in effect, operated a dollar standard, i.e., dollars have been most commonly used for international payments and as the main convertible currency. Therefore governments, banks and financial institutions outside the United States have been more than willing to hold US dollars. The resulting Euro-dollar markets have grown rapidly since the 1950s, creating a pool of international money and financial assets available to inflate financial markets open to international capital inflows. The political-economic factor has been the rise of funded pension schemes since the 1960s, investing pension contributions in capital markets, causing them to inflate. In the 1980s, the Austrian economist Josef Steindl referred to such inflation of the capital markets as enforced indebtedness of companies.[16]

Financial Inflation in Developing Countries

The developing and newly-industrialised countries, i.e., those countries outside the US, Canada, Australia and New Zealand, and North and West Europe, have suffered severe financial inflations since the 1970s. However, they have been affected by financial inflation in a way that is markedly different from the way in which such inflation operates in the advanced capitalist countries. An important difference arises out of the narrower scope of credit in the developing and newly-industrialised countries. Cash is used for most transactions in those countries. Only the wealthy, big businesses and government agencies use credit routinely for payments and financing purposes. Banking systems are therefore more vulnerable to the loss of cash and the possibility of being unable to satisfy depositors requests for cash. This may not matter if the central bank makes available unlimited quantities of notes and coins to its banks. But if the financial authorities voluntarily limit their note issue, then they may refuse to supply the banknotes that a bank may need.

The limiting of the note issue is usually done as part of a monetary policy to reduce price inflation or to control the money supply in the face of foreign capital inflows. Such capital inflows not only cause financial inflation but usually also set off a speculative investment boom in fixed capital and real estate. Where such an investment boom ends up providing incomes for employees who do not use the credit system to make payments, it puts notes and coins into circulation outside the banking system. In the extreme case where the central bank will not provide any additional money, for example, if the country has a 'currency board' and is only issuing local currency against foreign currency in the central banks' reserves, then banks may be vulnerable to illiquidity. If a bank in such a situation is unable to borrow cash elsewhere it may collapse, imitating the banking crises of the advanced capitalist countries in the nineteenth century.

Therefore, the concentration of the credit system around a relatively few wealthy individuals and institutions makes it more likely that any financial inflation, even if to finance productive investment, will lead to an outflow of cash from the banking system.

A second common problem of financial inflation is that many developing countries have undergone sometimes quite extensive industrialisation financed and sponsored by governments or banks. This is most notable in the countries that had Communist governments, but it also occurred with perhaps smaller government participation in countries in Latin America and East Asia. Such industrial development means that there has not been a build-up of financial assets, held by individuals or institutions, which would be the counter-part of the productive capital established in the economy. Often the financial counter-part of that capital is the foreign debt of the government incurred in the process of building up new industries. Companies in the private as well as the state sector have more or less bank debt, but, unlike companies in the advanced capitalist countries, they have little internal liquidity that they can use to finance temporary financial deficits. Any investment or extension of their business has to be done by raising additional finance through the issue of new financial liabilities, i.e., speculative or Ponzi finance. Additional capital is much more securely used to increase internal liquidity, repay debt, or engage in corporate restructuring and merger and acquisition activity, rather than for actual productive investment.

A third common problem in developing countries is that their rentiers and investment institutions are relatively small, reflecting the low average income of the population, and its very unequal distribution. Attempts have been made in recent decades to encourage the inflation of capital markets by promoting funded pension schemes in the developing and newly-industrialised countries. However, such schemes have inevitably been limited by the relatively small number of people in such countries who have stable, secure and well-paid employment. Since the 1970s developing countries have been encouraged to open their financial markets to international capital flows, following the theory that investment in developing countries is held back by a 'shortage' of savings, and foreign capital is an effective way of remedying that shortage. But, as was noted above, the international financial markets have been greatly inflated since the 1970s. The entry of foreign capital into a developing or newly-industrialised country's financial markets therefore leads to a much more rapid financial inflation in that country than it does in the larger financial markets of the advanced capitalist countries. The withdrawal of that capital then leads to a catastrophic deflation of those markets, such as the financial crises experienced in Mexico in 1995, East Asia in 1997 and Russia in 1998. Schumpeter had already noted the incidence of such crises under the gold standard in his *The Theory of Economic Development* which he published before the First World War.[17]

Where local corporations have easy access to the more stable, well-developed markets of the advanced capitalist countries, financial liberalisation may cause large local corporations to avoid raising finance in local capital markets inflated by foreign capital inflows. Instead, they may take advantage of an appreciation in the local currency (as foreign capital enters the local economy) to finance themselves in financial centres such as New York or London, through capital issues or Depository Receipts. Such additional external finance then introduces two additional sources of financial risk: the exchange rate risk that the local corporations' external financing will increase in domestic currency terms if that currency depreciates in relation to the currency in which the external financing is obtained; and the increased inflation and instability of the local capital market. This last would have been reduced with capital issues into that market by corporations. A local corporation can, of course, protect itself from such risks by devoting the capital raised abroad to financial activities abroad. But this is not the kind of productive investment envisaged by the advocates of financial liberalisation.

8

Asset Inflation and Deflation

Financial inflation leads to bigger balance sheets, both assets and liabilities. This creates a sense of prosperity, and self-congratulation on the part of bankers, financiers and finance directors of firms. Disillusion sets in when financial inflation fails. When deflation sets in it reveals the self-delusion of markets, habituated to apparently endless capital gains from asset inflation, and the self-delusion of economists, habituated to convenience thinking that attributed such inflation to a prosperous equilibrium among rational optimising agents such as they conceive themselves to be. Effective understanding must look beyond the delusions created by markets to the structural shifts in the markets that account not only for the crisis (which excludes most theories of equilibrium among rational, optimizing agents) but also for the years of financial boom (which excludes most disequilibrium/euphoria-based theories of financial crisis).

The crisis that broke out in 2007 is a crisis of asset inflation and collateralised lending. Asset inflation involves the rise in asset values. In the past this has been attributed to expectations of higher future earnings (in the case of capital market assets such as stocks or shares), or the scarcity of the asset (in the case of housing assets). Neither of these factors can satisfactorily explain the long boom in asset values that has affected the US and UK markets, and their abrupt end in 2008. Attributing them to some nebulous 'confidence' followed by a 'loss of confidence' reduces experience to perceptions of that experience, without identifying the factors that have created the experience. Providing a historical account (from deregulation to the sub-prime crisis) gives us just 'one damn thing after another' rather than the shifts in markets that cause them to rise and fall.

The structural circumstances that produced the boom and then the crisis are the inflow of credit into asset markets and the reversal of that inflow. Those inflows and the current outflows are part of the system of collateralised lending that prevails in the US and the UK. Collateralised lending means lending against asset values. This provides security for the lending bank, and therefore less risky lending. Such a lending model may be contrasted with a more traditional system of lending against future income that is the staple model in economics and finance textbooks. Lending against income is always subject to risk, because it involves estimating income in an uncertain future. As Adam Smith pointed out this is especially risky in new businesses, where entrepreneurs out of vanity are prone to exaggerate their prospective profits. Lending against collateral means that, if not paid back, the lender can take over ownership of the collateral and sell it to recoup the value of the loan. Accordingly, as long as loan values are below collateral values, loans are secure and interest charged is therefore conventionally less than for unsecured lending.

The most important collateral in economies with sophisticated financial systems is financial assets. For structural and policy reasons, the most important asset inflation in recent years has been in the market for financial securities. From the 1970s, this inflation was initially due to the proliferation of funded pension schemes, i.e., schemes in which money is taken out of earnings and invested in financial markets in order to provide future pensions. More recently, the inflation of the US financial markets has been due to the large trade deficit of that country. Because the US currency is the reserve currency for most of the world, and most international debt is denominated in dollars, this led to an accumulation of dollar reserves in countries that had trade surpluses (principally East Asia and commodity exporting countries like Russia and Brazil). Those reserves ended up in central banks that used them to buy 'safe' US assets, such as US Government bonds. In that process, those foreign central banks contributed to financial inflation in the US.

When more credit comes into the capital market than firms and governments are willing to take out of it by issuing new securities, prices of securities rise. But not all securities will rise equally. Short-term securities and bonds usually have the price at which they are repaid written into the terms of the bond. As the date of their repayment approaches, their market price converges on their repayment price. The market price of such bonds will only exceed that repayment price by a small margin reflecting any differences between the interest payable on such a bond, and the interest payable on equivalent new issues. Excess demand for new securities will therefore inflate most of all equities (common stocks) that do not have any fixed repayment value. Thus as pension funds and foreign banks inflated the markets, equity markets boomed.

Financial inflation changes the way in which the economy works through the impact of this inflation on corporations or companies financing themselves in the capital market. Corporations found that they could issue shares cheaply, not just because they could issue shares at a high price (relative to dividends). Buyers were willing to pay that high price because they came to expect an additional return in the form of capital gain not paid by the company but by future buyers in the market for the shares. As a result of the excess demand for shares, corporations issued capital in excess of what they need to finance their commercial and industrial operations. In the past, shareholders disapproved of the over-capitalisation of companies because it 'watered down' profits (i.e., a given amount of profits had to be shared among more shareholders), and directors avoided it because it made it more difficult for the directors to control the majority of shares at a company general meeting. However, today's shareholders are mostly institutions whose large diversified portfolios are sub-contracted to professional fund managers and rated on financial returns, rather than on their interventions in the running of companies. At the same time, new techniques of senior management remuneration have tended to replace profit-related pay with share price-related pay, through stock options. Along with new techniques of debt management, stock option remuneration has removed inhibitions about the over-capitalisation of companies. Excess capital has been used to replace bank borrowing with cheaper long-term capital. Replacing borrowing with shares also has the advantage that pre-tax profits can be made to rise by the reduction in interest cost. Where excess capital has not been used to reduce debt, it has been used to buy short-term financial assets. Alternatively, excess capital is committed to buying and selling companies. Hence the extended festival of merger and takeover activity and balance sheet restructuring that has characterised corporate finance since the 1980s.

The overall effect on banks of company over-capitalisation has been to make them more fragile. Before the 1970s, the largest, most reliable borrowers from banks were large corporations or governments. From the end of the 1970s, such corporations found that they could borrow much more cheaply by issuing their own bills (company paper) or directly from the inter-bank market. If banks want to hold company loans, they have to buy them in the market at yields that gave banks no profit over their cost of funds in the capital or money markets. The loss of their best customers has turned banks towards fee-related business in derivatives and debt obligations markets, and towards lending into the property market and to other risky customers that banks had hitherto been treated with much more caution. From the savings and loans scandals of the early 1980s, to the sub-prime market crisis since 2007, it is clear that banking has become more prone to instability.

In the household sector, the equivalent of capital market inflation is the inflation of the housing market. The removal of restrictions on housing credit (formally in 1986 in the UK, but much earlier informally) made it much easier to obtain credit for house purchase. The increased credit then allowed demand to drive up prices, and to continue to drive them up, with a temporary relapse at the beginning of the 1990s. As prices rise, the system redistributes wealth and capital gains from those entering the housing market, usually on somewhat lower incomes at the beginning of their careers, to those who have been owning real estate for a longer period of time, i.e., older home-owners usually with higher incomes at a more advanced stage of their careers. The system not only redistributes income and wealth from the asset poor to the asset rich. It also turns the housing market into a giant Ponzi scheme: The condition for the realisation of extraordinary capital gains by the asset rich is the willingness of those entering the market to indebt themselves more and more. Once rising house prices are taken for granted, then those entering the market with huge debts can console themselves with the prospect of corresponding huge capital gains if they can survive the purgatory of paying most of their income in debt payments. This is called 'getting onto the property ladder'. The political consensus since the 1980s has considered this to be the only proper solution to securing decent accommodation. For those excluded from home ownership the state has dabbled, largely ineffectually, in various schemes to expand the supply of low cost housing (i.e., housing you would rather not live in for the rest of your life) for 'first time buyers'.

The system of asset inflation was stabilised by two mechanisms. Businesses operated in the financial markets not so much to raise capital for productive enterprise or commerce, but in order to expand their balance sheets and move through various kinds of financing up to equity (or common stock) financing. The effective aim was to hold capital in excess of what was required to finance productive activities. Excess capital was then held in the form of liquid assets. Liquid assets are the best collateral for loans. Therefore holding a stock of liquid assets makes it easier for a company to operate in the financial markets and cope with temporary cash outflows from the business. In this way over-capitalisation made corporations more financially stable.

The other stabilising mechanism operated through the housing market. The rise in the value of their real estate and financial assets has induced a change in saving behaviour of the middle classes. Hitherto the middle classes saved more or less passively: Income was put into savings to support future consumption in retirement. Only among the small minority of the wealthy upper classes was wealth used as a substitute for income, with legacies and realised wealth being used to support current expenditure. From the 1980s onwards, active use of their balance sheets to generate cash flow became much more common among the propertied classes. Asset inflation allowed the emergence of an alternative 'welfare state of the middle classes' based on borrowing against rising asset values, or the sale of inflated assets. Private health care, fees for education, replacement income in periods of unemployment, have increasingly, among the middle classes, been accommodated by borrowing against wealth whose value has conveniently been rising much faster than current expenditure, or turning such wealth over in asset markets.

When assets are no longer largely held long-term, to be realised only on death or retirement, but come to be held more briefly, for capital gain purposes, their turnover inevitably increases. The more common use of debt or asset sales to pay for current expenditure has brought down overall saving rates in the household sectors of the United States and Great Britain to negligible or negative levels. This, in turn, meant that firms' expenditure on production and fixed capital was realised more effectively by companies in the form of sales revenue, without leakages into household saving.

The two stabilisers of over-capitalisation and housing-market financed consumption broke down from around 2006 onwards. In the capital market, the emergence of debt-financed equity funds, which bought out companies and transferred their debts onto the companies' balance sheets in order to re-sell the companies (and debts), transformed the process of capital market inflation. The trend towards equity financing was now converted into a process of placing on company balance sheets debts used to inflate the equity market. The greater indebtedness of businesses reduced their willingness to invest. In the summer of 2008, a number of companies, most notably the multinational steel company Arcelor Mittal, announced major reductions in their investment programmes. This contraction in corporate expenditure inevitably reduced the cash flow of the business sector.

In the housing market, there was clearly a limit to which young people, at the start of their careers, could indebt themselves, even with the prospect of capital gains in their later middle age. It is significant that the housing boom broke not where houses were most expensive, where capital gains may be said to have been the greatest, and hence where a speculative 'bubble' may have been most distended. The boom broke where incomes were lowest, in the sub-prime sector of the market, where the market in the asset was least liquid, and therefore excessive debt could only be serviced out of a low and unreliable income, rather than out of capital gain.

With a reduction in the credit entering the capital and housing markets, relative to the credit being taken out of those markets, asset inflation reverses into asset deflation. Collateralised lending now chokes off the supply of credit even further. The proportion of housing value that mortgage lenders will advance was reduced in 2009 to between 60% and 75%. This obliges purchasers to put more of their own money into house purchase. The higher deposit requirement has reduced the number of borrowers capable of meeting the standard for prudent collateralized lending. Moreover, with falling asset values, home-owners find that the excess of collateral value over outstanding loan value disappears, and may even become negative.

In a situation of asset deflation, debt which previously could be written off against capital gain, by turning assets over in their markets, must now be paid out of income. This creates a problem of excess debt in the economy which is forcing households to raise their savings rates, i.e., reducing the proportion of income devoted to consumption. While the official view and economic theory regard all saving as essentially voluntary, and hails it as facilitating investment, debt previously serviced out of capital gains, and now serviced out of income, is a form of 'forced indebtedness'. A firm or household forced to service debt out of income in this way will try to reduce that debt, rather than spending income or, in the case of a firm, rather than spending on new equipment. This is because such excess debt cannot be paid by selling assets, and its existence on the credit record of an economic unit makes it more difficult to obtain credit in the future.

By reducing current expenditure in this way asset deflation forces the economy into recession. Recession brings down the rate of inflation affecting current goods and services (measured by the consumer prices index, or the retail prices index, or even the GDP deflator). There is now an increased danger that prices of current goods and services will start to fall. If they fall, then debt deflation sets in, as falling prices increase the real value of debt in the economy: The greater the effort to repay debt, the more prices fall, and the more the real value of the remaining debt rises. In this way, as Fisher argued in the 1930s, attempts to repay debt are frustrated and the economy languishes in economic depression. If this happens then the economies of the US and UK are in for a very long period of stagnation and unemployment. Japan experienced fifteen years of debt deflation after 1991, when even the rapid expansion of demand in East Asia, before and after its crisis in 1997, and in the U.S. failed to stimulate a recovery.

Inflation in the economy as a whole, rather than just the financial markets, is the natural, non-catastrophic way of eliminating excessive debt in the economy: as everyone's incomes and prices rise, the real value of debt declines and debt payments become more manageable. The three decades since the 1970s were marked by intensive efforts on the part of central banks to eliminate inflation. Where this was achieved (usually through currency overvaluation, or some other means of cheap imports) it left no mechanism for eliminating excessive debts. Asset deflation turns excessive debts into bad debts. This is because lending against expected increases in capital values, where such expected increases turn out to be greater than actual asset inflation, leaves a margin of loans without security, and some borrowers without the means to repay loans. In this way the loss of capital gains has resulted in the deterioration of bank assets and generalised bank failure when mutual suspicion causes previously reliable inter-bank lending to dry up. In this situation, central bank policy is ineffective: lower interest rates cannot stimulate expenditure in a situation of excess debt, because of the preference to use any spare liquidity to repay excess debt. Buying assets from banks ('quantitative easing') or recapitalising them improves the liquidity of bank balance sheets and may stabilise asset prices. But that cannot make indebted customers borrow. In these circumstances, banks start to operate as 'zombie' banks: i.e., banks that can make payments (under government guarantee) or take deposits (under bank guarantee), but cannot lend, because no-one wants to borrow.

PART II
The Culture of Financial Inflation

9

Twentieth-Century Finance Theory: The Frauds of Economic Innocence

(in memoriam J. K. Galbraith)

Contemporary financial economics, like alchemy, is a calculating pre-science. It aspires to scientific status, but fails to achieve it because financial economics is driven by a search for its own philosopher's stone, and its theorists are distracted by the pursuit of red herrings. The philosopher's stone of finance is a method to forecast stock prices or, what amounts to the same thing, a way of speculating risklessly. This search is documented in a recent book edited by Geoffrey Poitras.[1] The volume is concerned with the twentieth-century 'discoveries' of Markowitz, Merton, Miller, Black, Scholes and other legends of academic finance who converted 'a collection of anecdotes, rules of thumb, and manipulations of accounting data' into 'a rigorous economic theory subjected to scientific empirical examination'.[2] By a process of restricting the arguments until a determinate algorithm for forecasting stock prices or determining risk emerges, modern quantitative finance offers the philosopher's stone, but substitutes for it 'optimal', 'risk-adjusted' portfolios that are only optimal or risk-adjusted in such a limited sense as to be impractical. Nevertheless, since only a saint or a subversive would ever settle for anything less than an optimal or risk-adjusted portfolio of wealth, the prospectus for quantitative finance inevitably wins out over more modest and more practical approaches. Our heroes secured valuable Wall Street consultancies. But they were employed largely for marketing purposes and were rarely allowed to influence actual investment practice and strategy.

Moreover, contrary to Merton's self-serving assertion, not all of the alternative approaches to finance are mere anecdotes, rules of thumb, or manipulations of accounting data. As Paul Davidson argues persuasively in the paper that concludes this volume,[3] the work of Keynes, and we may add his followers such as Minsky, was much more systematic and does not require such unreal assumptions about banking and financial markets. However, from the point of view of the 'finance discipline' Keynesian, Minskyan, and other such theories are handicapped in the market for academic and professional ideas by their positive realism, their search for insights into what is really happening, rather than the norms that they offer for successful speculation. (I would like to think that this is the reason why Paul Davidson and I are not on Wall Street payrolls.) Despite Merton's puff about 'scientific empirical examination', modern finance is normative in purpose and assumption, and has been interpreted as such by fund managers in its main markets in the US and UK.

Markowitz' portfolio theory was the first major red herring, postulating a universal calculus to obtain optimally diversified portfolios with spreads of returns depending upon the extent to which investors were willing to hold risky assets. It was but a small step to impose a determinate frequency distribution for future returns and divide those returns into a market average and a stock-specific return. Thus was born the Capital Asset Pricing Model that is the staple of the modern finance textbook.

Arguably the red herring that drew most academic hounds and spawned the most important subsequent red herrings was the Modigliani-Miller 'theorem'. Most readers of finance textbooks know this as 'proving' that the value of a company is independent of its financing. In fact, the theory shows that in a state of perfect competition and knowledge of future returns, financing does not affect the value of a company. Merton Miller's especial contribution to the theorem was not only the observation that there was a wide dispersion of financing between debt and equity among American companies, but also a very convenient definition of equilibrium in which no further arbitrage was possible. The theorem was most widely interpreted as demonstrating that any non-random distribution of financing among companies must be due to departures from the initial restrictive assumptions about perfect competition, knowledge etc. This set finance and economics off on a hunt for 'market imperfections' that may account for non-random financing.

An immediate consequence of this direction of reasoning was that corporate finance, or the study of how companies actually finance their activities, and the effects of that financing on their activities, disappeared from the discussion. Furthermore, with the assumption of 'no possible further arbitrage' the investigation of actual financial market processes was reduced to connecting prices to 'information'. All that was now necessary to understand markets was time series analysis of price data. Far from extending the boundaries of our knowledge, finance theory was now excluding key aspects of financial activity from the scope of its analysis.

The search for 'market imperfections' led to other theoretical innovations that further narrowed the 'scientific' and policy discourse of finance. Predictably, Chicago identified taxation and market regulation as the culprits in financial market inefficiency. In response, Stiglitz at MIT offered information asymmetries as causing financial market imperfections. At Yale, Robert Shiller offered behavioural finance (not mentioned in Poitras' book) and the failure of investors to calculate optimally as explanations of market inefficiency. By the end of the twentieth century, the key expenditure decisions of firms, that determine the dynamics of market economies, and the crucial influence of financing conditions upon those decisions, had dropped off the agenda of academic finance. Their residual trace on that agenda was Tobin's 'q' theory, relating the cost of investment to the cost of capital. But this was hardly seminal and, in its general equilibrium form, is relatively trivial.

The first part of this book discusses some of the theories pre-dating the quantitative revolution. Here Morgen Witzel examines the financial management ideas of Jeremiah Jenks, Edward Meade, and William Ripley[4]; Geoffrey Poitras introduces us to the ideas of Frederick Macaulay and Frank Redington[5]; and Gabriel Hawawini and Ashok Vora discuss how the calculation of yields evolved from the seventeenth century onwards.[6] In this part too, Robert Dimand contributes an excellent survey of Irving Fisher's contributions to finance theory, curiously omitting Fisher's debt deflation theory.[7] However, for reasons not made clear, Keynes's analysis is absent from this part of the volume. Keynes is discussed separately at the end of the volume in Davidson's contribution. This is possibly more logical because Davidson engages so extensively and enthusiastically in polemics against the general equilibrium foundations of quantitative finance theory. Keynes's appearance as an afterthought like this may also be connected with the concentration in this volume, in contrast to the first volume of Geoffrey Poitras' book, on developments in American finance theory.

Among the papers published here, 'The history of quantitative risk measurement' by Elton McGoun invites special mention because of its scholarly explanation of how, in the course of the quantitative revolution, uncertainty became conflated with calculable risk, and that calculable risk was then restricted to tractable frequency distributions into which historical price data could be more easily fitted. The 'results' of analysis came to dominate realism: '... anything that is "extremely difficult" is "avoided" as "hardly affecting the results"' (p. 207). The prophet of formalism in American economics, Wassily Leontief, had denounced this kind of intellectual sleight of hand which he identified with the (Keynesian) 'neo-Cambridge school'. But Milton Friedman had reassured everyone that such scruples are unnecessary because the only methodological requirement for theory is the ability to make testable predictions. McGoun provides a clear account of how, under a regime of such 'theoretical rigour', redefining terms allowed financial economists to persuade themselves that they were calculating the incalculable.

In the final analysis it is not possible to see where finance went wrong, or how it was reduced to providing sedative comfort for practitioners facing the usual unprecedented uncertainty in the financial markets,[8] without an overview of the history of the discipline, such as this volume, and its companion provide. In any discipline, individual papers and works invite criticism of their assumptions and/or their theoretical or methodological consistency. Only a survey of their history can give a clear indication of where an applied discipline such as finance has taken a wrong direction, or disengaged from the issues of our time, and the consequences of that disengagement. This is the main achievement of this volume and its editor Geoffrey Poitras assisted by Franck Jovanovic.

My only overall reservation about this book is that it tends to accept the Merton line that the emergence of quantitative finance has been a purely academic process of 'discovery'. This is very apparent in the middle part of this volume entitled 'The Modern Finance Revolution: The Inside Perspective', and in the final part entitled 'Alternative Perspectives on the Revolution'. In the first of these sections Hal Varian, Rene Stultz, Robert Jarrow, and Fisher Black pay glowing tributes to the intellectual profundity and originality of Markowitz, Miller, Merton, Sharpe, Black and Scholes.[9] In the third and final part, Franck Jovanovic, Donald MacKenzie, Elton McGoun, and Paul Davidson question the assumptions that underlie quantitative finance. This presents finance as an academic hermeneutic, finding and criticizing scholarly antecedents, and thrilling at or belittling originality. But behind these discussions was the depression into which the stock of investment bankers had fallen in the 1930s,[10] and the recovery in that stock with the process of inflation in the US financial markets from the 1970s onwards, to the point where it is now impossible to read Galbraith's classic, *The Great Crash* sensibly without choking on *déjà vu* at the chapter entitled 'In Goldman Sachs We Trust'.

The emergence of quantitative finance was associated with the rise to financial market pre-eminence of fund managers deploying huge investments in increasingly unstable securities markets. The previous system of stabilizing portfolios by holding government securities was losing its effectiveness with the repayment or depreciation of War debts, large capital issues by corporations, and a corresponding need to rebalance portfolios in favour of private sector liabilities. The theoretical innovations of Markowitz et al. offered a rationale for convincing fund managers that their portfolios were just as safe even as they were getting more risky. This background, mentioned only in passing in the editor's introduction, would naturally suggest a consideration of the macroeconomic consequences of finance, and the apparent inability of financial economists to see beyond their price data analyses. However, since this volume was published when the current liquidity drain in the markets was a mere gurgle in the upper intestine of Wall Street it is, perhaps, easier to overlook the absence of this consideration. Nevertheless, the outcome of that financial inflation in the US, and the abject failure of economists to provide a systematic account of it, makes this book so timely. Until economists and policy-makers emancipate themselves from mainstream finance theory, we cannot improve our failing financial system nor even start to create a scientific discipline of finance.

10

Fischer Black's 'Revolution'

There is a strong case for the view that everything of interest about the Nobel Laureates in Economics of the last two decades has already been proclaimed in the official biographies that accompany their awards. Perhaps for this reason, Perry Mehrling chose as the subject of his most recent book not Robert Merton or Myron Scholes, who were awarded the Nobel Prize in Economics in 1997, but their co-author Fischer Black, who died in 1995 and therefore could not share in their award because the Prize is never awarded posthumously.[1] Had he been alive and shared in the Prize, there is no doubt that a Nobel biography highlighting the 'scientific discovery' of the Black-Scholes option pricing formula would have captured all that was exciting about Fischer Black. Perry Mehrling's book demonstrates how much more can be said about someone whose life and career was as predictable as his acclaimed contribution to economics was uncontroversial.

Mehrling's attempt to invest Black with heroic qualities is perhaps the only major failure of this book. The son of a small-town businessman, Fischer Black's precocious ability in mathematics and computing brought him a scholarship to study physics and mathematics at Harvard. There, the famous American liberal university education ensured that he acquired no systematic knowledge of any subject in particular, but was able to dabble in social science and philosophy (he returned to the work of Willard Quine later in life). His main interest then was in the possibilities of using computers to develop artificial intelligence. In 1964, he was awarded a Ph.D. at Harvard for a dissertation in applied mathematics entitled 'A Deductive Question Answering System'. Then, as now, applied mathematics offered little in the way of a career, except perhaps for the boffins simulating war games for the Pentagon, but was of interest to banking and financial institutions at work in the post-War financial boom. Computing was expanding hugely the possibilities of organising systematically the securities price data that economists from Irving Fisher, through Alfred Cowles III (founder of the Cowles Commission) believed, if subjected to sufficient processing, would reveal how to beat the market, or at least how it could be predicted. Inevitably Black was drawn to consultancy work, initially for A. D. Little, and subsequently for his own consultancy firm, Associates in Finance, calculating whether and how the market could be beaten.

At A. D. Little, Black first met Jack Treynor. Treynor introduced Black to the Capital Asset Pricing Model as a way of thinking about securities prices. Briefly the model states that the return on a security, that essentially determines its value, consists of a return that is the average for the market in which the security is traded, plus some multiple of that return that may be greater or less than unity, and that is specific to that security. In some versions of the model, that security-specific multiple (known as 'beta', the return relative to the market return) is treated as an index of the riskiness of the security, so that it essentially measures the margin of risk offered by the security (and hence the excessive return) over the return from a risk-free security. In finance theory, the Capital Asset Pricing Model came to be associated with the 'efficient markets hypothesis' or the view that prices in securities markets reflect all the publicly-known information relevant to the evaluation of each security. Any relevant privately-held information comes into the market through the buying and selling that holders of such private information will undertake.

Black embraced these ideas with enthusiasm and, as Mehrling points out more than once, they remained a constant theme and inspiration in his work. No matter that they involved some peculiar assumptions, such as perfect arbitrage, and zero transactions costs. Black's first major finance assignment, for Wells Fargo Bank, was to develop a 'product' or investment offer that would give customers of the bank consistently higher than average market returns without higher risk. According to the efficient markets hypothesis, this was something that could only be temporarily and unpredictably achieved. 'Noise' traders who speculated on market inefficiencies should, over the long period, lose money to 'professional' traders who made the market efficient. Black nevertheless thought that he had found a stratum of securities whose risk was consistently under-priced. His proposal was rejected by the Wells Fargo's fund managers, because the active trading strategy that it entailed would have been too expensive.

The meeting with Treynor had other consequences. In 1969, Treynor became editor of the *Financial Analysts Journal*, a professional rather than academic journal. This became Black's main publishing outlet, allowing him to get his ideas into print without having to undergo the tedium of persuading academic journal editors of the value of his reasoning.

In 1971, Black obtained a visiting position at Chicago University that later was converted into a tenured chair. At Wells Fargo, Black had met Myron Scholes. Together they produced the options pricing formula, for which they became famous, even before Black came to Chicago. It was published in the *Journal of Political Economy*, Black's only paper in a highly ranked academic journal. The success of the formula was assured by personal connections with the Chairman of the Chicago Mercantile Exchange, Leo Melamed. Melamed had recognised the trading opportunity offered by the breakdown in financial regulation that had come with the collapse of the Bretton Woods system of fixed exchange rates. He used the coterie of free market economists at Chicago, headed by Milton Friedman, to argue for the liberalisation of regulations preventing options trading at his exchange. Once options trading started in 1983, the Black Scholes formula came into its own, since any option bid or offer price that deviated from the one indicated by the formula pointed to a speculative gain for the trader. Mehrling rightly points out that it was not the first such formula: Samuelson had published a 'Rational Theory of Warrant Pricing' in 1965. But the Black-Scholes formula was more general, and more convenient to use.

Mehrling does not go into the technicalities of the formula, so that the unreal assumptions, such as efficient markets and perfect liquidity, that Black and Scholes were obliged to make in order to arrive at their equation, are not really discussed in the book. Black did develop a more realistic version with fewer restrictive assumptions. But this attracted little attention, even in this excellent book. All of which goes to show that what the markets were after was a pricing convention, rather than an insight into reality. For a while, the Black Scholes formula performed well. But as other formulae emerged and came to be used by traders, the Black Scholes formula performed less well.[2]

An implication of efficient markets is that the study of financial markets gives one worldly experience, because all the 'relevant' information comes to the market. Most of those engaged in finance at a trading or a senior level, are naturally flattered by seeing wisdom in what the markets do, and in particular in the trading or strategic decisions of market participants. Study of this wisdom and the efficient markets hypothesis thus reinforce a delusion that the rest of the world is like the financial markets or, if it is not, then it should be. This was no less true of Fischer Black. His schemes to reform accountancy to orientate it towards giving a 'true' value for a company's stocks, pension finance (sticking to bond holding), or corporate finance, betray an almost touchingly naïve belief in market efficiency, and the efficacy of looking at financial positions as options. Even so, the insight into the operations of financial markets, promised by the capital asset pricing model and the efficient market hypothesis, turns out to be hopelessly unrealistic. Black's view that the 1987 Crash happened because investors' appetite for risk increased was a typical, *ex post* rationalising, implication of these theories. After he moved to Goldman Sachs in 1983, Mehrling reports, his quantitative trading schemes lost money. The bank's fortunes peaked in 1993 thanks to fixed income, currencies and commodities positions, rather than Black's trading.

So much for the conventional career and ideas. These were more symptomatic of, rather than determining, the rise of finance in US capitalism, that was, and largely remains, beyond the knowledge and understanding of most economists. As may be expected from the author of an outstanding book on US monetary policy,[3] Perry Mehrling brings to Black's work on economic theory outside finance a breadth that one could only wish that his subject had had. But about half-way through, the book reveals Fischer Black in an unusual challenge to conventional wisdom with the chapter on 'The money wars'. Black was largely self-taught in economics. He learned his economic theory by reading journal articles in between consultancy assignments, and through more extensive reading of Hayek during the 1980s. This education brought him right up to the cutting edge of economic theory as it was around 1933. His inability to get his papers on monetary theory, business cycles and general equilibrium published in academic journals was not just because of the faddishness and exclusiveness of journal editors. Nevertheless, this does not mean that Black was merely derivative in his economics. Some of his interventions do raise important issues for the economic theory of his time and today.

A case in point is his view on money. Even before he had arrived in Chicago, Black had disputed Milton Friedman's view that the way to control inflation and stabilise the economy is to regulate the money supply. Black's reasoning is revealing. According to the efficient markets hypothesis and the capital asset pricing model, traders are supposed to respond to changes in securities prices according to whether the traders are risk averse, or are willing to make a play for higher returns in exchange for higher risk. If securities prices rise, investors who are not averse to risk are supposed to leverage up their portfolios: borrowing more in order to invest in rising stock prices. In the same situation, and faced with an increase in the value of their risky assets, risk averse investors are supposed to sell securities and place the proceeds into risk-free bank deposits or government paper in order to maintain a constant proportion of riskless assets in their portfolios. However, if the supply of bank credit is inelastic, then the resulting market efficient general equilibrium cannot be obtained. Interest rates will rise as bank credit expands and thwart the re-establishment of an efficient equilibrium in the financial markets, that is, an equilibrium that reflects all the relevant information and the attitude to risk of the investing community. In other words, although Mehrling does not say so explicitly, endogenous money, or perfect liquidity – the possibility of costless and instant conversion of assets into current money – is a condition of maintaining efficient equilibrium. But if that is the case, as Keynes or Wicksell might have pointed out, then the rate of interest cannot be determined in the 'real' economy by the balance between saving and investment. In general, Mehrling points out, Black was hostile to any active monetary policy because it interfered with the general equilibrium established by what he regarded as the community's attitude towards risk.

Black's views on business cycles, much like his mature political views, were warmed-up Hayek, although Mehrling is too polite to say so. In Hayek's monetary business cycle, economic instability arises as different industries adapt to changed monetary conditions, with lower interest rates stimulating over-investment in more productive industrial processes that take longer and involve more industrial specialisation in the production of final goods. Black's criticisms of the 'real business cycle' theories of Kydland and Prescott were an apt reminder of the realities of industrial production, but unfortunately timed just as industrial economics was being displaced by finance theory. Black believed that the widespread assumption in real business cycle theory of equilibrium between flow variables ignored the active part in economic decision-making played by disequilibrium between stock variables, capital stocks in particular. Black nevertheless adhered to general equilibrium in a way that Hayek never did. Hence his rather odd view that the markets were in equilibrium during the 1987 Crash.

Finally, Mehrling highlights Black's critical attitude towards econometrics. Black defined econometric models as ones whose structure is defined by data, rather than theory. In his view, this led to serious misspecification in nearly all cases, with the result that estimated coefficients 'are virtually meaningless'.[4] In his second and final book, his starting point was 'stylised facts'. He listed twenty-three such facts, which he proposed as the subject of economic analysis. These were headed by 'unlimited growth', 'persistent inequality' and 'growing specialisation'.[5]

Throughout the book, Mehrling allays the reader's doubts about the intellectual significance of Fischer Black by showing his work as an honest intellectual response to increasingly dishonest times. This gives his book a fascination that cannot be attributed to any of the grey personalities he describes. One of the major strengths of North American economics is its continuing investment in the popularisation of economic ideas, as exemplified in the work of people like Douglas Dowd and Paul Sweezy, and journals like *Challenge* and *Monthly Review*. We had that too in the UK, as evidenced by John Stuart Mill's 'People's Edition' of his *Principles*. But we seem to have lost it with the shackling of academics to an insecure treadmill of teaching to improve the career paths of our students, and researching to impress other academics in the discipline, so that popular economic discourse is taken over by journalists with little interest in the consistency of ideas. Perry Mehrling has shown that it is possible to write a research-based book that can and will be widely read. It should be recommended to students in preference to those boring old finance textbooks.

11

Economic Inequality and Asset Inflation

In the discussion about the financial crisis since 2007, one important factor has been overlooked, namely the distribution of income and wealth. It is obvious that the social consequences of the financial crisis have been made so much more painful by the growing inequalities of income and wealth in the US and the UK that preceded the crisis. But there are also connections between such inequalities and financial instability. These have been highlighted by many critics of finance. For example, John Hobson, most famous for his 1902 classic *Imperialism: A Study*, argued that inequalities of wealth and income gave rise to over-saving, and hence economic stagnation. More recently, the late John Kenneth Galbraith noted the connection between tax cuts for the rich and asset inflation. Nevertheless few critical observers[1] have been able to go beyond the obvious and odious facts of increasing hardship alongside the conspicuous consumption and display of housing assets by the beneficiaries of financial inflation.

Asset inflation and income and economic inequalities are intimately linked. Asset inflation means rising values of financial assets and housing. Such inflation allows owners of such assets to write off debts against capital gains, buying an asset with borrowed money, and then repaying that borrowing together with interest and obtaining a profit when the asset is sold. Hence the proliferation of borrowing by households and consumption ultimately financed by debt. When the asset is housing, its inflation is especially pernicious because housing is such a basic need in all societies and among all classes. The profit that accrues to the owner of an asset from the appreciation in its value depends to a great extent on how long that asset has been owned.

The older owners therefore benefit most from an appreciation. The housing market then redistributes income and wealth from young people earning less at the start of their careers and indebting themselves hugely in order to get somewhere decent to live, to people enjoying highest earnings at the end of their careers. But housing inflation is also like a pyramid banking scheme because it requires more and more credit to be put into the housing market in order to allow those profiting from house inflation to be able to realise their profits.

Nevertheless, even those entering the system with large debts hope to be able to profit from it. Such has been the dependence of recent governments and society in general on asset inflation that the political consensus is 'intensely relaxed' about such regressive redistribution of income. That consensus has encouraged the belief that the best that young people can do to enhance their prospects is to indebt themselves in order to 'get on the property ladder', i.e., enrich themselves (or at least improve their housing) through housing inflation.

Those at the bottom of the income distribution inevitably suffer most from rising house prices because, living in the worst housing, they have the least possibility to accommodate their house purchase to their income by buying cheaper, smaller housing. Having little other option but to over-indebt themselves in order to secure their housing, default rates among households in this social group are also most likely to rise with house price inflation. This inequality lies behind the problems in the sub-prime market in the US and the equivalents of that market in the UK and elsewhere. Paradoxically, a more equal distribution of income and wealth is more likely to keep the housing market in equilibrium, because any increase in house prices above the rate of increase in income and wealth is more likely to result in a fall in demand for housing. Where income and wealth are already unequally distributed, and house prices rise faster than incomes, a fall in demand from those who can no longer afford a given class of housing is off-set by the increased demand for that class of housing among households that previously could afford better housing. In this way, the redistribution of income and wealth from those with more modest incomes to those with higher incomes also facilitates asset inflation in the housing market.

Thus asset inflation has increased inequalities of wealth and income and those inequalities have further fed that inflation. Such inflation is therefore a self-reinforcing pathology of financial markets and society, rather than, as the economics establishment tells us, a temporary disequilibrium (a 'bubble') in the markets. Financial stability rests not only on sound banking and financial institutions. It also requires a much more equal distribution of income and wealth.

12

The Wisdom of Property and the Culture of the Middle Classes

At the end of the twentieth century, while financial economists satisfied their intellectual pretensions to useful knowledge by conjuring up visions of a world peopled with materialistic consumer-investors optimising rationally in accordance with their willingness to hazard their wealth, the propertied classes succumbed to new delusions created by the financial markets. The reasoned response of propertied individuals to their experience of finance has created a new political culture with important consequences for the political economy of capitalism. The propertied classes of the past were a combination of landowners and rentiers, that is, owners of financial securities. The former were oppressed in most progressive countries by death duties and were made even more insecure by the declining real value of rents, that is, the value of rents in relation to the rising cost of maintaining the style and accommodation appropriate to a landowner. In their turn, rentiers had been made insecure by the financial crises and inflation that punctuated the progress of finance from the latter half of the nineteenth century and culminated in the 1929 Crash.

From the 1970s, the growing prosperity of the middle classes in the 'financially advanced' countries, such as the United States and Britain, was associated with a switch in their asset holdings, from modest holdings of residential property and direct ownership of stocks and shares, to residential property that was increasing in value and indirect ownership of stocks and shares in the form of funded pension entitlements and insurance policies. In the early 1960s, the majority of stocks and shares in both countries were owned by wealthy private individuals.

A decade later, the majority of stocks and shares were owned by pension funds and insurance companies. This does not mean that such funds were not active before the 1960s. They were, but had only a limited market because their use-value was just that they provided pensions and insurance. After the financial crises of the early 1970s, financial inflation gave such intermediary funds a new use-value: that of financial enrichment.

Pension funds and insurance policies are relatively illiquid, and the cash flow that they provide is restricted to circumstances provided for in the terms of the policies: pensions in retirement, or payments defined by the terms of an insurance policy. However, the long boom in the housing market, with its growing liquidity, allowed additional borrowing against capital gains in that market. In the United States from the 1970s, so-called '401' pension funds allowed contributors to draw out of those funds before retirement. Financial inflation and the conversion of capital gains into income change the way in which capitalism is experienced by those living in that system. That changed experience in turn alters the culture, preoccupations, and hierarchy within the propertied classes in the following ways:

a) *Humanity as an appendage of asset markets.*
As a consequence of labour market deregulation, income from employment has become more volatile and uncertain in the US and UK. Those who own property come to be dependent upon capital gains from asset inflation to maintain standards of consumption [see d) below] and secure a future with more precarious employment income. The prospects for inflation in asset markets take over a dominant part in the rational economic expectations of individuals with property, just as the prospects of acquiring property with the potential for appreciation in value comes to be the focus of the economic ambitions of those without property. Professional or career advancement takes a secondary place to the search for capital gains, as the bureaucracies of the welfare state are balkanised, so that public sector assets can be turned over in asset markets to realise capital gains and replace tax revenues in defraying the cost of public administration [see d) and f) below].

In the private sector itself, a new source of alienation emerges as production comes to be incidental to the much more lucrative business of balance-sheet restructuring. Vastly more capital can be turned over even more rapidly in the markets for property or financial assets while the pedestrian business of production is limited by techniques of production, and the relative difficulty with which such techniques may be modified. The value of any labour or effort becomes inconstant since, at any one time, it depends on an ephemeral conjuncture in the financial markets. A productive worker producing a value in excess of his or her wage, may still be negligible if the balance sheet on which he or she may appear as an asset may be sold for even more profit in the financial markets. The residual pride of the producer in the product or service in which her or his labour is embodied, a labour already fragmented by specialisation and capitalistic machine production, now becomes even more a melancholic nostalgia for medieval craftsmanship rather than a realistic attitude to work or professional ambition. The common factor in our humanity at work or at home comes to be our pre-occupation with asset values.

This new community emerges as politics, culture and history – the other sources of our common humanity – become private consumption choices or leisure activities, like the preferred television channels that 'private individuals' watch, or tracks that they download onto their MP3s; or collective consumption choices, like sports events or concerts; or the imagined history that people choose when they seek to ennoble their lifestyle by attaching their consumption choices to a particular tradition. These sad attempts to find relief from alienated labour or to realise a common humanity are doomed to eventual frustration precisely because they are private choices in a society whose members' only common preoccupations are debt and the opportunities for easing it with asset inflation. In this way, humanity is reduced to an appendage of asset markets; as under industrial capitalism, we were reduced to appendages of machines; as previously, under the absolutist state, we were appendages, once, twice or so many times removed, according to our place in the social hierarchy, of the throne; or as, even earlier, in the medieval theocracies, the altar gave us our community. Our dependence on banking and financial markets defines our common humanity as did our earlier dependence on the throne or the altar.

This social dependence is reinforced by the prior claims that debt has on everyone's income and wealth. Businesses and business individuals may go out of business, bankrupt themselves, in order to avoid their creditors. But for the reasoning individual with a non-financial life, such balance sheet restructuring disrupts the pursuit of personal, family or professional advancement through which we find satisfaction and respect in our communities. As long as asset markets are rising, debt is easily managed and we can all, with the exception of the asset-poor, proceed with satisfying our personal or social ambitions. When asset markets fall, human advancement is set aside in the effort to reduce debts in the same way that the feudal peasant left his land and family in order to work on the land of his lord. In a society bound by property contracts and asset markets, the road to serfdom goes through finance.

b) *The social hegemony of investment bankers.*

As financial markets inflate, their apparent success contrasts with the lagging performance of under-invested industry. At this stage, far from concentrating resources on industrial renewal, financial innovation concentrates on mobilising financial resources to sustain rising asset prices: *in an era of finance, finance mostly finances finance.* The concentration of financial resources on purchasing financial assets and the extension of credit for such purposes results in financial inflation. Such inflation establishes the reputation of investment bankers whose decisions and advice are responsible for the concentration of resources on buying financial assets. The resulting financial inflation is then attributed to their superior insight and their knowledge of which assets will enjoy increases in prices.

Such superior insight is of course a delusion, as Keynes showed in his famous analysis of investment behaviour.[1] Once investment bankers agree on the assets that are most likely to appreciate in value, and summon up the buying power of the investment funds that they advise, those assets inevitably will appreciate. Such appreciation confirms the genius of investment bankers who can lead a sufficiently large pack of fund managers into the purchase of particular assets. But the source of their success lies in their ability to concentrate buying, rather than in any ability to identify objective growth prospects. In asset markets, such prospects are not inherent features of particular assets, but reside solely in the minds of market participants.

A more real accomplishment of a good investment banker is the ability to refinance balance sheets in order to convert notional capital gains into cash flow. Such refinancing is easy while financial markets are being inflated and attracting liquidity. The investment banker can then literally take the credit for turning capital gains into money that the market as a whole is attracting in pursuit of such gains. Obtaining such cash flow is by no means so easy when asset prices fall. This concentration on balance sheet restructuring narrows the worldly experience of bankers and financiers. Nevertheless, the dominance of financing arrangements in household, government and company affairs makes practitioners in finance increasingly sought-after policy advisers. In this capacity, their *deformation professionelle* inclines them even more to providing a standard solution of balance sheet restructuring to complex social and economic problems.

c) *An enhanced delusion of successful thrift among the middle classes.*

In any scientific study of economic behaviour in market economies, it is necessary to distinguish the experiences or perceptions that people may have, from the market process that gives rise to such experiences or perceptions. Individuals who enjoy the benefits of asset inflation only directly experience the purchase of the financial asset which gives them a claim on a capital gain, rather than the money coming into asset markets that allows that gain to be realised. Capital gains are therefore 'naturally' attributed to provident and well-calculated asset purchase, perhaps even to some intrinsic characteristic of a given asset, rather than generalised asset inflation.

In this way the propertied classes succumb to a comforting illusion, carefully cultivated by their financial advisers and intermediaries, that their foresight and financial acumen have secured them their gains.

In fact, the situation is quite the reverse. The benefits which the propertied classes obtain from inflated property and financial asset markets are increasingly capital gains on wealth rather than accumulated saving out of income. As property markets inflate and pension funds mature, it is the propertied classes who dissipate on their own consumption the capital gains that they are able to take out of property and financial asset markets through the enforced saving of the young buying accommodation at prices that swallow up most of the incomes of the young or lower paid workers obliged to subscribe to pension funds.[2] The delusion of thrift reinforces a growing sense of financial self-reliance and independence of the state welfare system.

d) *The emergence of inflated property and financial asset markets as a 'welfare state of the middle classes'.*
Inflated asset markets act as a welfare state in that such markets socialise the financial liabilities of those owning such assets. Asset markets afford asset owners relatively unconditional access to money through the sale of an asset typically to another asset owner with spare liquidity or borrowing against the value of the asset. Inflated asset markets allow owners of such assets to cross-insure each other in this way against extraordinary liabilities for health care, holidays, school fees, the purchase of housing, or the repayment of inconvenient debt. Such extraordinary liabilities may be accommodated by taking out of those asset markets money that is being put into them by those acquiring such assets. This has the political consequence of alienating those with property from a state welfare system for which they pay but from which they derive little benefit. This disconnection lies behind middle class taxpayers' demands to reduce the cost of that welfare state by concentrating state benefits more narrowly on 'those in need'. In its turn such concentration reinforces that middle class alienation from the state system.

e) *The marginalisation of those without appreciative wealth.*

They may be homeowners in places where wealthy property-owners do not wish to buy housing, or without claims on inflating assets, such as housing, in places where wealthy property-owners are buying housing. Where property-owners transfer capital into the housing market, the increase in house prices obliges the young and migrant workers to live in over-crowded conditions, because housing has become a perquisite of property-owners, rather than being available to all. Not having property denies marginalised sections of society the opportunity to operate balance sheets actively: debt is more likely to finance current consumption, rather than the acquisition of inflatable assets. These are the lower class counterparts of those among the propertied classes whose possession of inflated assets allows them to consume in excess of their incomes. An unequal distribution of income is thus enhanced by a growing distinction between the 'balance sheet' rich, and the 'balance sheet' poor.

f) *State-administered social welfare as a system for prosecuting the poor.*

While the official welfare state may provide some minimum income for those without means of support, this is at the cost of taxpayers predominantly among the middle classes. Such minimum income is increasingly delivered with a degree of institutional bullying and hectoring, designed ostensibly to make welfare claimants more active in securing their financial independence but, in reality, designed to reassure propertied tax-payers that those claimants are being penalised for their improvidence in not having property to support them. It is not, as politicians and economic advisers repeatedly assert, a question of the claimants' 'willingness to work': no-one threatens the propertied classes with removal of their income for their improvidence in living on unearned income from property or capital gains on that property. The selective penalisation of those without property or income is a natural consequence of a state welfare system that is no longer comprehensive because the middle class is increasingly opting out of it.

g) *The delusion of risk-taking.*

The asset rich attribute their superior capital income to 'risk-taking'. This is a delusion because the asset-rich have their financing and income hedged by assets, and a hedged risk is no risk at all, or a purely subjectively perceived risk. The biggest risks are undertaken by the asset-poor because their financing and income are not hedged by assets and an unhedged risk is a real one. When financial markets are being inflated, the structure of rewards in the different trades and professions is such that those who take the lowest risk, because they hazard other people's money, get the highest rewards; while those who take the highest risks, because they entrust their meagre savings to financial intermediaries with the least possibility of hedging the hazarding of those savings by those intermediaries, obtain the lowest rewards.

Financial inflation is therefore no mere temporary departure from equilibrium in a standardised model of capitalism. It changes the character of capitalism and the range of choices that firms, individuals and households face. An enhanced option to consume without income is bought at the cost of financial instability, industrial decadence and regressive social values.

PART III
Financial Crisis

13

Everything You Need to Know about the Financial Crisis but Couldn't Find Out Because the Experts Were Explaining It

What a Credit Crunch Means

The financial crisis is referred to as a 'credit crunch' so widely now that many people associate the term with any bank collapse. In fact, the term 'credit crunch' has a very specific technical meaning. A credit crunch arises when banks or financial institutions have lent money due for repayment in the distant future, but are financing those loans with short-term borrowing which cannot be rolled over (i.e., repaid out of new short-term borrowing). There are various reasons why banks may wish to finance long-term lending with short-term borrowing. One of these might be that the interest rate on short-term borrowing is much lower than the rate on long-term lending. But the common reason for this kind of financing in the two years before the crisis has been the difficulty that banks have had in selling off their long-term loans packaged up as bonds (see securitisation below). Under the current system of bank regulation (the so-called Basle Accord), banks with long term loans on their balance sheets are required to hold additional bank capital in case the loans go bad. Banks that could not sell off loans packaged up as bonds were transferring those loans into off-balance sheet subsidiaries called 'special purpose vehicles' financed by short-term borrowing. When the inter-bank money markets stopped lending in the summer of 2007, banks with special purpose vehicles found themselves with large amounts of short term borrowing due to be repaid, but without the ability to re-borrow in order to pay off that borrowing.

A credit crunch is a liquidity problem. It simply requires an agency, like a central bank, to lend money to enable banks to continue to operate until their loans are repaid. A liquidity problem needs to be distinguished from a solvency problem, where a bank's assets are less than its liabilities so that, if liquidated, the bank could not pay all of its obligations. The difficulty for bank regulators is that solvency problems in practice are indistinguishable from liquidity problems. Insolvent banks usually eventually experience illiquidity while even a solvent bank, if liquidated, may not be able to repay all of its obligations, because the prices of assets are usually reduced by their forced sale.

However, in the present crisis there are other, serious structural problems in banking and financial markets that are responsible for the crisis. These are:

Asset Inflation

Asset inflation means rising values of financial assets and housing. Such inflation allows owners of such assets to write off debts against capital gains, buying with borrowed money, and then repaying that borrowing together with interest and obtaining a profit when the asset is sold. Hence the proliferation of borrowing by households and debt financed consumption. Housing inflation is a particularly pernicious phenomenon, because it redistributes income and wealth from young people earning less at the start of their careers and indebting themselves hugely in order to get somewhere decent to live, to people enjoying highest earnings at the end of their careers. But it is also like a pyramid banking scheme in that it requires more and more credit to be put into the housing market in order to allow those profiting from house inflation to be able to realise their profits.

Nevertheless, because eventually even those entering the system with large debts hope to be able to profit from it, the political consensus is 'intensely relaxed' about such regressive redistribution of income and encouraged the belief that financial markets can do no wrong.

Those at the bottom of the income distribution inevitably suffer most from rising house prices because living in the worst housing they have the least possibility to accommodate their house purchase to their income by buying cheaper, smaller housing. Having little other option but to over-indebt themselves in order to secure their housing, default rates among households in this social group are also most likely to rise with house price inflation. Paradoxically, a more equal distribution of income and wealth is more likely to keep the housing market in equilibrium, because any increase in house prices above the rate of increase in income and wealth is more likely to result in a fall in demand for housing. Where income and wealth are already unequally distributed, and house prices rise faster than incomes, a fall in demand from those who can no longer afford a given class of housing is off-set by the increased demand for that class of housing from among households that previously could afford better housing. In this way, the redistribution of income from those with more modest incomes to those with on higher incomes also facilitates asset inflation in the housing market.

As asset inflation increases inequalities of wealth and income those inequalities further feed that inflation. Such inflation is therefore a self-reinforcing pathology of financial markets and society, rather than a temporary disequilibrium of asset markets.

Risk Management

Risk management by banks and financial institutions in 1940s and 1950s consisted in holding vast amounts of government paper that other banks and central banks would always buy in at a good price. Much of this government debt was eliminated by inflation in the 1970s and the 1980s. Government obligations were replaced in bank and financial institutions' portfolios by private sector (household and firm) liabilities. Financial theory put forward new techniques of risk management by portfolio diversification and derivatives. However, this does not eliminate risk, but merely spreads it around other portfolios. As the poet John Donne might have said 'no portfolio is an island, intire of itself', as is assumed by modern portfolio theory.

Securitisation

Since the 1980s, banks kept their portfolios of long-term loans liquid (i.e., convertible into money) by bundling up debt into bonds that they sold to institutions. More bad debt meant giving more guarantees, or buying someone else's guarantees through credit default swaps, or credit insurance. As these bonds became more difficult to sell, they were increasingly held in subsidiary special investment vehicles (s.i.v.'s, originally set up to manage the payments on mortgage bonds). Passing loans into subsidiaries like this has made bank balance sheets opaque: no one knows the true scale of the financial liabilities of any bank. With asset prices falling, banks have every incentive to pass their risky debts into such subsidiaries. Moreover, having insured and reinsured each other's risks through derivatives such as credit default swaps or credit insurance, every bank is exposed directly or indirectly to every other banks' risks.

The Elimination of Inflation

The liberalised credit market generates excessive debt, especially with asset inflation, when banks, competing for profit, will lend against future increases in asset values, rather than solely against future income. Inflation in the economy as a whole is the natural, non-catastrophic way of eliminating excessive debt in the economy: as everyone's incomes and prices rise, the real value of debt declines and debt payments become more manageable.

The three decades since the 1970s were marked by intensive efforts on the part of central banks to eliminate inflation. Where this was achieved (usually through currency overvaluation or some other means of cheap imports), excessive debt resulted in bad debts. This is because lending against expected increases in capital values, where the expected increase turns out to be greater than actual asset inflation, leaves a margin of loans without security. Some borrowers, who might have planned to repay their debts by selling appreciated assets, or who might have planned to refinance their debts using capital gains as collateral, find themselves unable to refinance or repay their debts in full by selling assets. This leaves them without the means to repay loans. When asset prices stop rising altogether, or fall, this loss of capital gains can result in generalised bank failure.

Structures Determine Crisis

The above outline describes the situation in North America and Great Britain. Not every financial crisis is the same. The financial difficulties in other countries arise out of structural features that are often peculiar to those countries. In Iceland, for example, capital market inflation allowed banks to issue lots of capital, which was then invested in lending to 'entrepreneurs' buying companies abroad in the expectation that capital market inflation would also increase the value of their holdings in those companies. Banks 'hedged' their lending against foreign currency securities by taking in large amounts of foreign currency deposits, making themselves vulnerable to the withdrawal of those deposits.

In Eastern Europe, as elsewhere, banking systems differ from country to country. But they have certain features in common which affect the crisis mechanism of particular countries. A common feature is foreign ownership of banks, ranging from around half in some countries, such as Poland, to virtually the whole of the banking system in Estonia or the Czech Republic. Foreign bank ownership drains the inter-bank money markets of a country. Even in a country like Poland, where money markets are active, they are in fact an artificial market for central bank deposits, activated by central bank open market operations. This makes the banking systems of Eastern Europe particularly vulnerable to the changes in the credit policy of foreign banks, such as raising their risk margins because of the apparent fragility of banking in general.

In Eastern Europe too, central banks were obliged to take a narrow view of their responsibilities, focusing solely on inflation. High interest rates encouraged the over-valuation of Eastern European currencies, such as the Polish zloty and the Hungarian forint. In turn, these circumstances encouraged widespread borrowing in foreign currencies. The peculiarity of excessive debt in Eastern European lies in the fact that a large proportion, in some countries the majority, of household debt is in foreign currencies. This exposes households not only to increasing debt, as their domestic currency depreciates, but also to rising interest rates as foreign banks raise risk margins on their lending to Eastern Europe.

Eastern European banks which have lent in foreign currencies, financing their lending by short-term borrowing in foreign money markets, are vulnerable to illiquidity as they face repaying that short-term borrowing from further borrowing, or by buying foreign currency in the foreign exchange market on such a scale as to cause further depreciation of the domestic currency. As real estate markets experience falling prices with the withdrawal of credit by foreign banks, even mortgages in domestic currency become more risky and less secure.

The Problem of Excessive Debt

Excessive debt is the major structural link that causes crisis in the banking system to spread out to the real economy, i.e., the economy outside the financial markets. Excessive debt is simply the debt that households and firms owe and would rather not have. They therefore try to eliminate it by repaying it. In this way, the amount of credit in the economy is reduced. Economic activity is curtailed because income is not spent on goods and services, but taken out of the economy to repay debt. The crisis was transformed into a general economic crisis in the summer of 2008 when a large number of indebted companies, which were expecting to convert their borrowing into shares (a much more stable form of financing because shares do not have to be repaid, and payments on them, i.e., dividends, are discretionary) found that they could not refinance their borrowing in this way. In large part, this was because the market for new share issues was wholly taken by the recapitalisation of banks. The large companies responded by cutting their investment, effectively reducing the sales of suppliers of investment equipment and their workers.

Unfortunately the problem of excess debt has been little discussed among economists and bankers, where the prevailing model of credit suggests that all borrowing is 'voluntary'; i.e., borrowing which people and firms willingly undertake and whose risks can be diversified away, or 'hedged' by derivatives, so that there is no urgent need to repay it.

Recapitalising banks, as governments are doing around the world, will not resolve this problem. Giving banks more capital can merely enables those banks to continue operating as 'zombie' banks: fulfilling their normal payments and deposit functions, but unable and unwilling to lend because the excessive debts that they hold in their portfolios are depressing the activity of the real economy. The problem is not banks' unwillingness to lend, as policy-makers in Britain seem to believe. The difficulty is the desire of people and firms to reduce their debts when they can no longer manage their debts through asset inflation. When asset prices are falling, the only way in which debts can be reduced is by cutting back on expenditure, or by selling depreciated assets, or by not reinvesting in the financial markets money returned on the maturity (repayment) of loans. The last two measures reduce the value of financial assets.

This problem is complicated by the unequal distributions of income and wealth. Most households and most firms do not have enough assets to be able to operate effectively in the financial markets. They will therefore cut their expenditure. The result of reduced expenditure is a depression that will continue as long as firms and households feel the need to repay debts. This is why the crisis is more than just a bank failure.

14

The Limitations of Financial Stabilisation by Central Banks

This essay discusses the instruments available to central banks for stabilising financial systems in the face of international capital mobility. These instruments are control of the money supply and credit availability, the short-term rate of interest, and open market operations. None of these instruments can be more than temporarily effective and, with financial innovation and inflation, they are less capable of independent use. The essay explains that these instruments are powerless against financial instability because world financial systems are divided into two mutually incompatible monetary systems: those based on a government bond standard; and those based on a foreign currency reserve standard.

Introduction

Emerging market crises since the 1990s have highlighted the role of international capital movements as mechanisms bringing about financial inflation and then, by the withdrawal of that capital, triggering the collapse of vulnerable markets. At the root of all this is a distribution of productive capital around the world that does not match the distribution of expenditure. Therefore the *national* units or *currency* areas, across which cross-border expenditure or capital flows take place, rarely have balanced cross-border expenditures or capital flows but tend to suffer from chronic deficits or surpluses.[1] In the Bretton Woods era before 1971, limited financing of deficits was available through the offices of the International Monetary Fund. Since then, the international financial stability has depended upon securing private capital inflows to finance current account deficits. In their turn, private capital inflows are necessary to stabilise the exchange rate of deficit countries. The problem that arises is that for most countries such international capital inflows are unsustainable, and hence countries with current account deficits periodically experience debt and exchange rate crises, which destabilise other countries by depreciating the financial and economic assets in crisis-affected countries, and by reducing demand in them.

It is fashionable to blame the governments in the countries affected for these crises for corruption and inappropriate fiscal and monetary policies, such as financial 'repression', excessively low real interest rates, or unrealistic exchange rate pegs. Such features may be in the background of particular crises. The trouble is that they tend only to reveal themselves *ex post* in a crisis. There are, however, other structural characteristics of private capital movements which arguably could cause crisis even if the most appropriate government policies are in place. Private financial (portfolio and short-term bank) capital inflows are usually unsustainable because they entail accumulative foreign financial liabilities whose withdrawal may merely be postponed by financial inflation. Other private capital inflows in the form of foreign direct investment by transnational companies depend on the ephemeral liquidity of international investment funds and multinational companies.

Stabilising such capital inflows by central bank action tends to be problematic because of the size and the changing motivations for such inflows. The size of the capital flows tends to require the concentrated use of all the instruments that a central bank has at its disposal. This then leaves no instruments free to be deployed in pursuit of other policy objectives. Hence the tendency in recent years of central banks in emerging markets to concentrate on the priority of stabilising their capital inflow. Only central banks in countries of reserve currencies, such as the United States, or in countries protected by controls over capital inflows, such as China or India, can enjoy the luxury of being able to pursue other policy objectives, such as low inflation, economic growth, financial stability, etc.

Limitations of Central Bank Instruments

Central banks have three instruments that they can use and have recently started using a fourth. They can attempt to control the money supply by varying the reserve requirements of banks and their own supply of those reserves. This has recently fallen out of fashion because there is little evidence that it actually limits the supply of credit when banks can buy reserves in inter-bank markets, or obtain reserves at little or no additional cost from the central bank.[2] When there is a foreign capital inflow, control of the money supply requires additional sterilisation operations: the sale of bonds, or an increase in banks' reserve requirements. In particular, control of the money supply may be used to manage the *consequences* of a capital inflow. It does nothing to control that capital inflow directly, although the advocates of the monetary theory of the exchange rate could argue that it may indirectly affect capital inflows through the effect of the money supply on the exchange rate. According to the theory, excess monetary expansion is supposed to leave too much money in pursuit of foreign currency, leading to exchange rate depreciation. Such a depreciation would of course discourage foreign capital inflows, but may be necessary to sustain the profitability of export trades.

A second instrument is the use of central bank interest rates to attract or discourage foreign capital inflows. This is not easy to do, partly because the ability to attract or discourage capital inflows depends on the rate of interest *relative* to interest rates elsewhere (and this only under conditions of financial stability). Moreover, the margin between domestic interest rates and foreign interest rates that may be necessary to attract foreign capital depends on the risk perceived by international investors. If this fluctuates, then so must that margin. However, notwithstanding a long period of its expansion since the 1980s, international financial liquidity can also fluctuate. When it is reduced, as it was for a while around the turn of the century, even higher interest rates may not be sufficient to attract foreign capital, especially if higher interest rates are perceived as entailing higher risk.

Finally, the effect of higher interest rates on the stability of corporate finances should not be ignored. If foreign capital account transactions have been liberalised, and interest rates have been raised to attract a foreign capital inflow in order to stabilise the exchange rate, then large local companies can reduce interest costs by replacing local borrowing with borrowing in foreign currency. This increases the vulnerability of large companies (which undertake the bulk of private sector fixed capital investment) to an eventual exchange rate depreciation if the attempted stabilisation proves unsuccessful.

The third instrument which a central bank may use is open market operations. The limitation of this instrument is that it may have little effect beyond the financial markets. In a time of financial inflation and financial innovation in particular, the counter-parties to the central bank's open market operations may offset elsewhere in the markets the desired effects of such operations. For example, the sale of government bonds to reduce bank liquidity may be off-set by banks' sales of securities to replace that liquidity. In emerging markets, the sale by a central bank of long-term securities to sterilise a foreign capital inflow can be made ineffective by such off-setting transactions. In more financially advanced countries, where financial inflation and innovation have limited the scope of central bank interest rates, open market operations are increasingly used just to enforce those rates across a wider range of financial instruments.

One implication of the reduced effectiveness of open market operations in respect of the liquidity of the banking system, is an increased effectiveness of such operations on the liquidity in the markets for the securities which are being bought and sold by the central bank. If government bonds are sold to reduce the liquidity of the banking system, and banks restore the liquidity of their balance sheets by selling bonds in the stock market, then this reduces the liquidity in the stock market. In this way, through its open market operations, the central bank may influence the liquidity of the capital market. This is of crucial importance at a time when the inflation of capital markets, and their recent deflation, is a major determinant of the liquidity of corporate balance sheets and hence their willingness to invest in fixed capital and new technology.[3] The liquidity of the capital market is furthermore a key factor in currency convertibility, which is the central problem of the international monetary system.

In recent years, a fourth instrument has started to be used. These are 'swaps' by which one central bank 'swaps' its currency for currency supplied by another central bank. The US Federal Reserve agreed such a swap arrangement with the European Central Bank soon after the Euro was set up and further 'swap' facilities were agreed with South Korea, Mexico and Brazil in the wake of the financial crisis. Other regional swap agreements, whether formal or informal, exist between other central banks.

The problems here are usually political. Swap arrangements involve the exchange rate of a currency being underwritten by a central bank in a more powerful country. As long as this is seen as being mutually beneficial, it works. But such agreements are vulnerable to disagreements over other aspects of central bank policy. The recent politicisation of finance and money raises new challenges for such agreements.

Two Systems of Convertibility

The convertibility of a currency has been at the heart of monetary economics since the origins of such intellectual enquiry. In the days of the gold standard, convertibility into that monetary standard was supposed to ensure the maintenance of the value of money. The use of gold in international transactions facilitated trade between countries whose currencies were convertible into gold. The loss of this convertibility with the fall of the gold standard was therefore associated with inflation and the decline of international trade.[4] Since 1971, there has been no universally accepted standard of convertibility. Exchange rates have fluctuated. The inflation that marked the two decades following the demonetisation of gold confirmed the worst suspicion of advocates of a monetary standard. This is that, without such a standard, inflation is inevitable. However, the effects on international trade were minimal because a lively trade in foreign exchange markets ensured that international payments could be made, at least by traders in the major trading countries.

The low inflation since the 1990s and the continued growth of international trade does not mean that the issue of convertibility has been resolved. The existence of different degrees of convertibility of currencies (irrespective of the *rates*, or prices against each other, at which they are convertible), from the US dollar to the inconvertible currencies of economies largely closed to international capital flows, suggests that the issue has become more complicated rather than resolved. The distinction between 'reserve' currencies and non-reserve currencies, with the latter convertible in varying degrees against the former, raises the question of precisely how those reserve currencies acquired and hold that status.

At this point many economists resort to politics, history and psychology. Politics suggests an answer that the US dollar is universally accepted because the United States is the most powerful country with the largest economy in the world. This may be true, but a currency is not usually held because of the political qualities of the country in which it was issued, unless tribute is being exacted from the rest of the world in that currency. However, in a world of market exchange, it is the structure of that exchange rather than feudal tribute which privileges some currencies. History provides an answer that, in the immediate post-War period, other currencies had to be exchanged for US dollars and only those dollars could buy foreign currencies. However, that was two generations ago, and does not explain why the US dollar is still the main reserve currency of the world. In a world in which currencies can lose their convertibility virtually overnight, the enduring convertibility of the US dollar cannot be explained by its situation over thirty years ago. Psychology provides an answer that, like paper money in domestic circulation, holders of US dollars have 'confidence' in that currency and are therefore willing to hold it. This is a circular, *ex post* argument: we only know that central banks and international banks have 'confidence' in the dollar because they hold it, and they hold it because they have 'confidence' in it. The significance of that confidence remains obscure because the evidence for that confidence is what that confidence is supposed to explain. In this way the knowable is reduced to the unknowable, which does not really elucidate the question.

In fact the real reason for the emergence of an international monetary system stratified into reserve and non-reserve currencies is the operation of two systems of convertibility in the world. Most central banks in the world issue currencies whose convertibility depends on their holders being able to effect an exchange for imported foreign currencies. In this respect, their currencies operate like those of non-gold-producing countries in the era of classical political economy: the standard of convertibility is a commodity which is imported, and the money supply that is convertible into that imported commodity at a fixed rate is limited by the amount of that commodity that is imported. With an international credit system, import of that standard of convertibility is somewhat more elastic than in a purely mercantile system in which the balance of trade determines the import or export of foreign currencies. However, at best this can merely smooth out fluctuations between trade deficits and surpluses: chronic trade deficits lead to foreign indebtedness, and the breakdown of convertibility. Because of this, securing capital inflows to balance chronic trade deficits can only stabilise the exchange rate temporarily.[5]

There is, however, another system of convertibility at work in the structure of international finance that operates in the countries of reserve currencies. This is a mechanism of convertibility that is dependent for its effectiveness on the ability of holders of that currency to convert it into a range of financial assets in that currency at a stable *rate* of exchange for those assets, i.e., at stable prices for those assets. This is the case with the United States dollar. In other words, the reserve status of that currency depends on the ability of holders of that currency to convert their currency into financial assets of a stable dollar value. The internal value of that dollar, i.e., the rate of price inflation in the United States is not a factor because foreign holders of dollar securities are more directly affected by price inflation in their own currencies. As for the external value of the dollar, i.e., its exchange rate against other currencies, this is only a factor if holders of dollar securities need an income in some other currency. On the whole holders of foreign financial securities are either wealthy individuals conspicuous for *not* being in need of immediate income, or else financial institutions with diversified portfolios who can meet immediate cash flow needs without having to sell depreciated assets. (An exception to this is discussed below.) Even economic decline and financial crisis may fail to reduce the value of this standard of convertibility if, as in recent years in the US, the crisis results in an *increased* demand for government bonds.

Thus it can be argued that the reserve currency status of the US dollar is due to the availability of a wide range of securities that may be bought with dollars. Should the outlook for US business worsen, then Treasury securities of stable value may be held, and indeed the demand for them ensures that their prices do not fall as the prices of corporate securities fall. In this way, good securities in the US dollar are nearly always available. This is how the dollar has sustained its position as the key currency in the international financial system.

Maintaining convertibility into long-term financial assets means keeping the capital market liquid. This is not a problem in circumstances of financial inflation, in which money inflows in excess of net new securities issues turn over more rapidly in the capital market. Any temporary illiquidity may be alleviated by the open market operations of the central bank, if the central bank buys in stocks. However, even this depends on keeping the capital market inflated over the longer term. If the economy moves into recession at the same time as the capital market deflates, then keeping the currency convertible against long-term securities becomes problematical. The situation of Japan is a case in point. With the capital market deflating, the Bank of Japan is in effect to monetising the bonds that its government is issuing to finance the deficit with which that government is hoping to reflate the economy. At the same time, the Japanese central bank is buying in (monetising) corporate securities to provide liquidity to the banks.

Conclusion

The important conclusion that can be drawn from this discussion is that no standard recipe for monetary stability or crisis management is appropriate in all countries. Developing countries and semi-industrialised countries with chronic trade deficits need to secure capital inflows to finance their trade deficits. The management of those inflows requires different tactics of central bank intervention to the tactics required to stabilise capital outflows from such countries with trade surpluses. These tactics have to focus on maintaining stable rates of convertibility of domestic currency for imported foreign currency. In the more financially advanced countries, the need for external financial liberalisation arises because of the need of financial investors to diversify their portfolios. Here the more important requirement is to maintain stable rates of convertibility of money against long-term financial assets. This then ensures that currency is willingly held abroad because it can be used to buy a range of remunerative financial assets. In this latter case open market operations ensuring the liquidity of capital markets come much more to the fore.

The tactics of central bank intervention also need to be differentiated because the problems that arise respectively under these two systems of convertibility are also different. In the case of countries operating on a foreign currency standard, the main danger is that of insufficient capital inflow, or a capital withdrawal, giving rise to an Argentine-style emerging market crisis.[6] In the case of countries whose currencies are on a financial asset standard, the most serious danger is that of financial deflation, which makes the long-term financial assets of a country unacceptable as substitutes for the currency of that country. In that case, holders of that currency, or bank deposits in that currency, have only the alternative of exchanging that currency for some other currency. This would then precipitate an exchange rate crisis.

A third conclusion concerns the compatibility of the two systems of convertibility. A naïve theory of international relations would suggest that if a common problem is perceived, then governments co-operate to manage or resolve that problem. However, in the case of two systems of convertibility, the fundamental problems are essentially different. The monetary authorities in countries on a long-term securities standard are most concerned to prevent the deflation of markets for long-term securities, and are less concerned about exchange rate stability. Monetary authorities in countries on a foreign exchange standard are most concerned about exchange rates stability. To obtain that, they need the co-operation of the monetary authorities in the financially-advanced countries. The effective co-operation of those central banks in the financially advanced countries is unlikely because monetary authorities operating a foreign exchange standard have little to offer in the way of support for the stability of long-term securities markets in the more advanced countries.

Finally, it is important to bear in mind the limited powers of central banks over monetary conditions in a country. These limitations tend to be obscured by the kind of categorical claims that are made in the literature on behalf of particular 'systems' of central banking, whether they are 'independent', or pursuing a Taylor Rule, or inflation targeting.[7] In particular, central banks can do very little in the face of private capital outflows, or financial deflation. Both of these are inevitable because the private capital inflows and the financial inflation that precede them entail accumulative financial liabilities. It so happens that the private capital inflows are often more short term, while the capital market in recent decades has been inflated by longer-term pension fund liabilities. Although private capital inflows are more obviously unsustainable because foreign capital withdrawal crises happen more frequently, financial inflation is also unsustainable. It just takes longer to become so.

15

International Business and the Crisis

The economies of most countries in the world are dominated by international businesses. Even though they may only employ a minority of the labour force, multinational companies dominate foreign trade. Crucially, their investments determine the pace and direction of business investment in most countries. In turn this investment determines the economic dynamics (rates of growth of output and employment) and the rate at which an economy acquires new technology and modernizes its economic infrastructure. In the present economic crisis, multinational companies are therefore a key institutional mechanism by which the financial crisis becomes a generalised economic crisis. But the way in which these mechanisms work has also been affected by changes in the financial system.

Generalisation about how the current financial crisis will affect international business, or multinational companies, is nevertheless a perilous undertaking. Multinational companies tend to specialize in particular industries. All of these industries are subject to cyclical fluctuations that tend to be peculiar to each industry, although we are now about to see these cycles coincide as particular economies and regions succumb to generalized economic depression. Furthermore, multinational companies do not all operate equally across the whole world. Their operations are usually concentrated in particular regions with links to particular financial centres. While many of these financial centres are more or less affected by the financial crisis, not all regions in the world are affected by that crisis. For example, India and China remain to date (the end of October 2008) relatively unaffected by the crisis, although this does not mean that they will not be affected in the future. Because of this differential geographical impact of the crisis, it will affect multinational companies differently according to where their operations and their financing may be concentrated.

Perhaps the only generalization that can be made about international business today is that it enters the present period of crisis and instability in remarkably good financial condition. As a result of the stock market inflation of recent years, large corporations have all raised capital in excess of their commercial or industrial requirements. Such excess capital is usually held as short-term financial assets (banks deposits, commercial paper) or else as holdings of shares in other companies. Certainly by comparison with banks in general, and many banks operating multinationally, international business had, at the time when the crisis broke, strong balance sheets and mostly good margins of solvency.

But it is in the nature of their business that multinational companies are mostly concerned about size and global presence. While financial markets were liquid, it made little difference to the overall liquidity of multinational companies to hazard their liquidity in merger and takeover activity to increase their size and global presence. However, as financial markets froze up in 2007, many multinational companies found themselves with large short-term financial market obligations which they were unable to refinance.

Moreover, even those multinational companies that have kept their margins of solvency in the form of liquid assets, find that these margins are now draining away as households raise their saving rates: household saving means that money which the business sector throws into circulation in the economy, in the course of production and exchange, does not come back to businesses as sales revenue. Fiscal deficits would normally increase the net income of the corporate sector, because they represent expenditure on goods and services produced by businesses that does not come out of the expenditure of those businesses. But these fiscal deficits are increasingly directed towards refinancing banking systems. The reserves of the business sector, built up from capital gains on assets such as palatial headquarters buildings, will be reduced as asset prices fall. Falling fixed capital investment in the financially advanced countries, and in China, whose investment has powered the recent industrial and commodity booms of many countries, will further cut the net income of businesses. International businesses, although in a strong position in many markets, will not be able to avoid the consequences of the contraction of those markets. Postponing new investment projects will only further squeeze new income for other businesses.

In this situation even businesses that manage to avoid substantial falls in sales because of their size and the scale of their international operations will be inclined to hold on to liquid assets rather than investing. But firms can only do this at the expense of other firms' sales revenue. So, while international business is in a better position to ride out the forthcoming recession than most smaller businesses, it will also contribute more than most towards creating that recession by withholding more expenditure than most. The crucial transition occurred in the summer of 2008 when a number of multinational companies such as Cemex, Tata Steel, Rio Tinto and Arcelor Mittal found themselves unable to refinance debts incurred in the process of major merger and takeover activity. They responded by cutting back drastically on their investment in productive capacity. Lakshmi Mittal may save money by cutting the capital expenditure of his international steel company Arcelor Mittal. But the suppliers of his capital equipment will lose that revenue, and those capital equipment manufacturers also use prodigious amounts of steel in their production. In any case, the rationale for investment is weak when a fall in global steel demand of 20 per cent and more is expected.

A second consequence of the international financial crisis that will undoubtedly affect international business will be capital controls. It is very clear that many countries will now adopt or strengthen controls on foreign capital inflows and outflows in order to stabilize their financial systems. In the past, foreign capital controls would have brought disapproval from the multilateral agencies charged with policing the international financial system, the International Monetary Fund, the World Bank, the OECD, and behind them the United States – disapproval reinforced by the threat of exclusion from IMF-led financing. But this was because past crises were international banking crises that these agencies hoped to resolve by refinancing bank debt through the capital markets.

Not only has the international climate of opinion towards capital controls changed. As before, the financing capability of the IMF is limited by comparison with the financing requirements for alleviating the crisis. The IMF is therefore acting as a lead agency to facilitate other sources of finance. However, since the other sources have been frozen up by the crisis, an important element in the additional financing have been central bank swap facilities that have been extended by the US Federal Reserve to central banks in Mexico, Brazil, and South Korea. In Europe, the European Central Bank has extended such facilities to central banks in Hungary, the Czech Republic and other new member states. In the case of Iceland, such facilities are being provided by Scandinavian central banks. Such assistance is being targeted on particular favoured countries in difficulty. But because much of the banking systems in the beneficiary countries, in many cases most of the banking system, is multinational, a more benign view is likely to be taken of capital controls. Capital controls would be necessary to prevent multinational banks from drawing down central bank assistance in a country benefitting from such swap facilities in order assist bank subsidiaries in another less favoured country.

Capital controls will tend to freeze the present hierarchy of multinational companies if only because competitors or potential competitors will find it more difficult to finance mergers and acquisitions in a declining capital market. It is a staple of business school research that most mergers and acquisitions do not improve the financial results of the companies being combined in this way. The rationale for mergers and acquisitions was in fact provided by capital market inflation, which made buying companies for resale at a higher price in an inflating market a profitable business proposition. This possibility no longer exists because of the large falls in the main stock markets of the world. Worse, most multinationals have their stocks quoted on more than one major stock exchange. This means that selling pressure frustrated by falling prices in one market is transmitted to other markets. Stockholders unable to sell a sufficient amount of stock in one market, because of the effect that this may have on prices, will distribute their selling across more than one market. Frustrated selling pressure will also frustrate the selling of new stock. The resulting inability to raise finance simultaneously in a number of countries will act as an informal capital control. The days of the multinational business that made money from restructuring its balance sheets in different countries is at an end. The prospects for making money in the more traditional way of production and technological innovation are not good.

Hitherto, inflating asset markets dominated by investment bankers earning *pro rata* fees for balance sheet restructuring has provided a very congenial ambience for international business theories that can provide some managerial rationale for such restructuring. Declining asset markets will be correspondingly uncongenial for such theories. Falling profits will reduce the supply of successful companies providing case studies of the 'excellence' attributed to alleged 'competitiveness', 'capability', 'internal advantage', 'synergy', 'competences', or some other mystical source. Furthermore, financial austerity will make it much more difficult to secure financial backing for management strategies driven by speculative theoretical projections. Financial asset inflation was the source of much of the financial success of international business and the most common means by which international business could emerge and thrive. For those researching the problems of international business, the only effective approach to understanding such business, the crisis provides an unrivalled opportunity to uncover the true constraints that determine the character and dynamics of cross-border capitalism.

16

Developing Countries in the Crisis Transmission Mechanism

As the financial crisis spreads out from its crucible in the US and UK, it has given rise to considerable discussion about its impact on developing countries. The situation itself is novel because previous international financial crises, the Third World Debt Crisis of the 1980s and the emerging market crises of the 1990s, spread *from* developing or emerging markets, so that developing countries were incriminated and affected from the start.

In the present crisis, the developing countries, for once, were not in the room when the crisis broke. Given the immense range of economic circumstances and exposure to international financial markets among the developing countries, the manner in which they are being affected is inevitably going to be more complex and indirect than in previous crises.

Current economic theory gives little guidance as to how the crisis will impact upon the developing countries. This is partly because the starting point of mainstream economic theory is optimization based on setting policy parameters that will secure internal and external equilibrium for a given country. It is more realistic to use a stock-flow analysis that places developing countries within a given structure of international economic and financial flows which are largely determined by expenditures in rich countries. Within this framework, assets and liabilities are largely determined by the history of past market disequilibria, rather than saving or portfolio preferences.

A key feature of the international monetary system within which the developing countries find themselves is that it is effectively an indirect US Government Bond Standard, in which the US dollar acts as a standard of value for all other currencies, and is held because it is directly convertible into US Government Bonds.

The nearest alternative international currency, the Euro, cannot take over as a reserve currency because a more or less balanced trade account does not allow the Euro-zone to supply the rest of the world with the amounts of 'free' (i.e., unencumbered by borrowing) Euros necessary to finance trade. Moreover, the ruling policy doctrine in the European Union remains hostile to government bond issues on a scale and liquidity that would be necessary to back a global reserve currency.

A second key feature of the international financial system is the means of payment for international transactions. These means are not US dollar banknotes, backed by the US Government through the US Treasurer and the Secretary of the Treasury who sign those banknotes, but commercial bank credits backed by bank loans to firms and governments. (Private individuals do not borrow in any significant amounts from international banks.)

Thus international banking has its counterpart in an international debt system, mostly in US dollars, whose net debtors are mostly smaller and poorer countries, because larger and richer countries can finance more of their needs with internal debt rather than borrowing from abroad.

Finally, crucial to the current structure of international trade and finance is the location in the US of the main markets for the commodity exports on which depends the foreign trade of most developing countries. Those commodities are therefore priced in US dollars.

These features of international finance and trade combine to make developing countries extraordinarily vulnerable to the financial crisis that is unfolding in the US in particular. As that economy succumbs to debt deflation (reduced expenditure in an effort to repay debt), imports into the US will be reduced, and with that the supply of 'free' dollars to the rest of the world. The other industrial countries, which are the main suppliers to the US, still have large domestic markets and are therefore less exposed than developing countries to a fall in their exports.

For the developing countries the reduction in their exports to the US has been exacerbated by the fall in commodity prices. However, that fall in commodity prices has been to some extent offset by the almost 30 per cent appreciation of the US dollar in foreign exchange markets since the crisis started.

This wholly unexpected appreciation has surprised many observers still thinking in terms of a foreign exchange market determined by rational portfolio calculations of varying degrees of risk-aversion. But the appreciation was entirely rational in the context of an indirect US Government Bond Standard.

However, that appreciation has been of little benefit to developing countries because they are the principal net debtors in the international financial system. Nearly two thirds of all international debt is denominated in US dollars and its value has therefore risen along with the appreciation of the dollar.

The US is of course the largest net international debtor in the world. But, because the international financial system uses an indirect US Government Bond Standard, the US Government can borrow abroad in dollars, servicing that borrowing in the same way that governments finance their domestic debt.

Foreign currency debt (net of foreign currency reserves) is therefore concentrated in developing countries and emerging markets. In this situation, monetary policy does not provide any solutions. Depreciation of the developing country's local currency against the dollar, to raise the domestic value of exports, increases the domestic cost of external debt financing. Pegging the exchange rate to the dollar holds external financing costs constant, but leaves the country exposed to reduced US dollar commodity export prices. Lowering the cost of foreign currency in local currency (i.e., appreciation) reduces export earnings, and encourages imports.

Since the turn of the century, the developing countries and emerging markets have done well out of the combination of a weak dollar and high commodity prices. While weaker commodity prices have been to some degree offset by the appreciation of the US dollar, that appreciation has also driven up the value (relative to the value of exports) of those countries' foreign debts, just as exports to the US are falling. This is the point at which the crisis puts financial pressure on poorer countries to add to the squeeze on their exports.

Epilogue

Does the World Economy Need a Financial Crash?

The title article of this collection suggests that a financial crash is preferable to a long process of debt deflation. A temporary failure of banking institutions may have less adverse impact on the economy than an extended period in which households and companies – in the case of households, burdened by excessive debt due to the inflation of the housing market, and in the case of companies, equity funds and merger and acquisition activity forcing companies into debt – use significant parts of the incomes to reduce their debt. Such debt deflation means that money which firms throw into circulation in the process of production and exchange does not all come back to them in the form of revenue, because households and other firms use it to repay debt. The resulting financial deficit of private business requires financing with further debt. In effect it becomes very difficult to escape excessive debt.

My title article suggested that the non-catastrophic, market alternative to debt deflation is a policy of inflation, ensuring that the growth of prices and wages is sufficiently high to reduce debt to more manageable proportions. But despite the bold claims of central bankers, it is not they who control inflation with their monetary policy, but inflation that controls central banks. The much-vaunted 'inflation-targeting', the policy of focussing monetary policy entirely on managing inflation, is simply a kind of 'reaction function' by which inflation makes central bankers behave in a particular way (raising or lowering interest rates) rather than a mechanism for regulating inflation. As the experience of Japan since the 1990s has demonstrated, governments and central banks do not have the control of inflation that is often ascribed to them.

Since the crisis started, the innovative policies that have been pursued by the Federal Reserve and the Bank of England under the name of 'quantitative easing' have involved buying bank assets from them in exchange for reserves. This has bloated the balance sheets of these two central banks. The purpose of the policy is to stabilise commercial bank balance sheets by making those balance sheets much more liquid, and through this getting the financial system to resume 'normal service'. But what was this 'normal service'? In the years up to the crisis in 2007 it was a process of credit expansion backed by asset inflation. This is what created the crisis, by indebting households and firms which could 'hedge' their debts with asset inflation. Unless that asset inflation re-emerges to accommodate excess debt, households and firms will continue to try to repay their excess debts out of income. The official policy therefore depends on reigniting asset inflation. But such inflation itself depends on an expansion of credit being placed into the asset markets by firms and households. With the recent experience of excess debt so vivid in their minds, firms and households are hardly likely to co-operate with such a strategy.

The other innovative measure that is being discussed, but has yet to be implemented, is regulation to increase the amount of capital that banks are obliged to hold. The reason for this is that the present fixed capital to risk-weighted asset ratios, originally agreed in Basle at the end of the 1980s, are pro-cyclical in the sense that in the course of an economic boom the liquidity and net worth of balance sheets increases. The fixed capital ratio that banks have to maintain therefore fails to discourage banks' risky lending and may even encourage it because the risks would be less apparent in the boom. The policy of requiring banks to raise capital ratios as a boom proceeds is sometimes referred to as 'dynamic provisioning'.

The flaw in this policy is that it does not take into account the situation in the capital market, where the supply of capital from the long-term investing institutions that dominate that market is inelastic, that is, pension funds and insurance companies can only invest in equity capital a relatively limited amount of their portfolios determined by insurance and pension fund regulations. Overcapitalising banks therefore leaves less capital available for industrial and commercial firms, and obliges those firms to use debt instruments or bank borrowing in place of capital. Capital adequacy regulations therefore cause excess debt, and hence cannot be a part of its solution. 'Dynamic provisioning' would require banks to drain the available pool of equity capital even more rapidly than under fixed capital ratios, causing a corresponding greater indebtedness on the part of companies, and forcing up even more the cost of capital that non-financial firms could issue. Far from stabilising banks and the economy, dynamic provisioning would destabilise the economy and the credit system, including banks, by indebting companies more rapidly in a boom, or else discouraging company investment. By these means, raising banks' capital requirements actually increases the risk of companies' default on their debt.

The other way to prevent financial bubbles is through the strict regulation of credit, of the kind that existed in the 1950s and the 1960s. But even this is open to various practical and social objections. In the first place that regulation failed, which was why the regulations had to be loosened in the 1970s and 1980s.

Secondly, and at best, it might eliminate credit fluctuations. But it could not eliminate the industrial business cycle, such as obtains in Germany and which has made Germans envy the freer credit markets of the Anglo-Saxon countries. Some of this envy is quite justified: if credit markets are less regulated, then it is possible to ease stagnating industrial performance with credit expansion backed by asset inflation. Effective credit regulation may therefore be expected to bring into public debate a coalition of banking and financial interests. This coalition will find more than one economist to testify that social welfare is best served by financial deregulation, so that we do not have to put up with the pedestrian and hazardous business of progress through the industrial cycle. They would find a ready public audience among the middle class, the 'asset rich' who are hardly ready to forego the anti-depressant dose that comes from observing that their assets have gone up in value again, affording a greater capacity to service debt and thereby making their debts and future consumption more secure. It is not clear that the middle class is ready to abandon the path marked out for it by the Chinese mandarin class who gambled their way to Revolution in the first half of the last century. The coalition of financial interests and economists will be there to reassure the asset rich that financial inflation can stabilise the economy, as it did in the US and the UK for two decades before the 2007 Crash. That coalition will be right. And the resulting Crash can always be blamed on governments, or even the spendthrift middle classes themselves.

Within the existing economic and financial institutions there is therefore no alternative to a Crash in which debts are wiped out. Avoiding it is merely prolonging the deflation of the economy. The true alternative is a system of economic organisation that avoids industrial *and* financial instability. It is time once more to consider socialism.

Notes

Introduction

1 J. Toporowski *The End of Finance: The Theory of Capital Market Inflation, Financial Derivatives and Pension Fund Capitalism* London: Routledge 2000, p. 7.

2 J. Steindl 'The Dispersion of Expectations in Speculative Markets' in *Economic Papers 1941–1988* London: Macmillan 1990, pp. 371–375.

3 J. Toporowski *The Economics of Financial Markets and the 1987 Crash* Aldershot: Edward Elgar 1993.

4 The review appears in pages 388–394 of *The Collected Writings of John Maynard Keynes: Volume XI Economic Articles and Correspondence Academic* edited by Donald Moggridge, London and Basingstoke: Macmillan, and New York: Cambridge University Press 1983.

Chapter 3: Neo-Liberalism and International Finance

1 League of Nations, *First Interim Report of the Gold Delegation of the Financial Committee* (Geneva: League of Nations 1930).

2 W. A. Brown, *The International Gold Standard Reinterpreted 1914–1934* (New York: National Bureau of Economic Research 1940), p. 801.

3 Over a century ago Hobson condemned the use of 'the public purse…for private gain', and the use of 'public resources' as 'the pledge of private speculations', J. A. Hobson, *Imperialism: A Study* (London: George Allen and Unwin 1938, first published 1902), pp. 97 and 59.

4 S. Strange *Casino Capitalism* (Oxford: Basil Blackwell 1986).

5 R. Brenner, *The Boom and the Bubble: The US in the World Economy* (London: Verso 2002).

6 J. E. Stiglitz *Globalization and Its Discontents* (London: Allen Lane 2002).

7 J. Grahl and P. Lysandrou, 'Sand in the Wheels or Spanner in the Works? The Tobin Tax and Global Finance' *Cambridge Journal of Economics* Vol. 27, No. 5, September 2003, pp. 597–621.

8 J. Toporowski. 'The End of Finance and Financial Stabilisation' *Wirtschaft und Gesellschaft* 29 Jahrgang 2003, Heft 4.

Chapter 4: Financial Innovation: Better Machines for Financial Inflation?

1 See S and K Aaronovitch, *Crisis in Kenya* (London: Lawrence and Wishart 1947).
2 H. C. Emery, *Speculation on the stock and produce exchanges of the United States*, (New York: Columbia University Press 1896).

Chapter 5: The Inflation of Goodwill

1 See next essay.

Chapter 6: Leverage and Balance Sheet Inflation

1 This is further explained in J. Toporowski, Notes on Excess Capital and Liquidity Management, Working Paper No. 549 (Annandale-on-Hudson, New York: The Jerome Levy Economics Institute of Bard Colleges November 2008).
2 See Irving Fisher 'The Debt Deflation Theory of Great Depressions' *Econometrica* Vol., No.1, pp 337–357.

Chapter 7: Inflation in Financial Markets

1 See essay 4 in this book.
2 J. M. Keynes, *The Collected Writings of John Maynard Keynes Volume VI A Treatise on Money Volume 2: The Applied Theory of Money*, London: Macmillan for the Royal Economic Society, 1971, p. 135.
3 R.G. Hawtrey, *A Century of Bank Rate* (London: Frank Cass 1962).
4 J. M. Keynes *A Treatise on Money in Two Volumes. 1: The Pure Theory of Money* (London: Macmillan & Co. 1930).
5 I. Fisher, *Booms and Depressions* (New York: Adelphi Company 1932).
6 F. A. Hayek, *Prices and Production* (New York, Augustus M. Kelly edition 1967).
7 R. G. Hawtrey *Good and Bad Trade* (London: Constable 1913); K. Wicksell, *Interest and Prices*, English translation (London: Macmillan 1936).
8 V. Chick, 'The Evolution of the Banking System and the Theory of Saving, Investment and Interest' in V. Chick, *On Money, Method and Keynes, Selected Essays* edited by Philip Arestis and Sheila C. Dow (London: Macmillan 1992); N. Kaldor, *The Scourge of Monetarism* (Oxford: Oxford University Press 1982).
9 C. P. Kindleberger *Manias, Panics and Crashes: A History of Financial Crises* (London: Macmillan 1989).

10 J. M. Keynes, *The General Theory of Employment, Interest and Money* (London: Macmillan & Co. 1936).

11 M. Kalecki, *Theory of Economic Dynamics: An Essay on Cyclical and Long-Run Changes in Capitalist Economy* (London: George Allen and Unwin 1954).

12 H. P. Minsky, *Stabilizing an Unstable Economy* (New Haven, CT: Yale University Press 1986).

13 H. P. Minsky, *John Maynard Keynes* (New York: Columbia University Press 1975).

14 I. Fisher, 'The Debt Deflation Theory of Great Depressions' *Econometrica* vol. 1, no.1, (1933): pp.337–357.

15 J. Toporowski, *The End of Finance: The Theory of Capital Market Inflation, Financial Derivatives and Pension Fund Capitalism* (London: Routledge 2000).

16 J. Steindl, 'Saving and Debt' in A. Barrère, *Money, Credit and Prices in a Keynesian Perspective* (London: Macmillan 1988).

17 J. A. Schumpeter, *History of Economic Analysis* (London: Allen and Unwin 1954).

Chapter 9: Twentieth-Century Finance Theory: The Frauds of Economic Innocence

1 G. Poitras (ed.) *Pioneers of Financial Economics Volume 2: Twentieth-Century Contributions* (Edward Elgar 2007)

2 R. Merton, *Continuous Time Finance* (Oxford: Basil Blackwell 1992), pp. xii–xiv, cited more than once in Poitras' book.

3 P. Davidson, 'Understanding Financial Market Prices: Reality vs. Rigour' in G. Poitras (ed.) op. cit.

4 M. Witzel, 'Early contributions to financial management: Jeremiah Jenks, Edward Meade and William Ripley' in G. Poitras (ed.), op. cit.

5 G. Poitras, 'Frederick R. Macaulay, Frank M. Redington and the Emergence of Modern Fixed Income Analysis' in G. Poitras (ed.), op. cit.

6 G. Hawawini and A. Vora, 'A Brief History of Yield Approximations' in G. Poitras (ed.), op. cit.

7 R. Dimand 'Iving Fisher and his students as Financial Economists' in G. Poitras (ed.), op. cit.

8 J. Toporowski, 'Mathematics as Natural Law: An epistemological critique of formalism in Economics' in M. Desai, S.C. Dow and P. Arestis (eds.) *Methodology, Microeconomics and Keynes Essays in Honour of Victoria Chick* (London: Routledge 2002).

9 H. Varian 'A Portfolio of Nobel Laureates: Markowitz, Miller and Sharpe'; R. Stultz 'Merton Miller and Modern Finance'; R.A. Jarrow 'In Honor of the Nobel Laureates Robert C. Merton and Myron S. Scholes: A Partial Differential Equation that Changed the World';

F. Black 'Robert C. Merton and Myron S. Scholes' all in G. Poitras (ed.) op. cit.

10 See Sweezy, P.M. (1941) 'The Decline of the Investment Banker', Antioch Review Spring, reprinted in Sweezy, *The Present as History* (New York: Monthly Review Press 1953): pp. 192–195.

Chapter 10: Fischer Black's 'Revolution'

1 P. Mehrling, *Fischer Black and the Revolutionary Idea of Finance* (Hoboken, NJ: John Wiley and Sons 2005).

2 J. Toporowski, *The End of Finance: The Theory of Capital Market Inflation, Financial Derivatives and Pension Fund Capitalism* (London: Routledge 2000): pp. 98–99.

3 P. Mehrling, *The Money Interest and the Public Interest* (Cambridge Mass.: Harvard University Press 1997).

4 P. Mehrling, *Fischer Black and the Revolutionary Idea of Finance*, op. cit., pp. 118–9.

5 P. Mehrling, *Fischer Black and the Revolutionary Idea of Finance*, op. cit. pp. 281–3. See F. Black, *Exploring General Equilibrium* (Cambridge, Mass.: MIT Press 1995).

Chapter 11: Economic Inequality and Asset Inflation

1 For example, Lankester, T. (2009) 'The Banking Crisis and Inequality' *World Economics* Vol. 10 No. 1.

Chapter 12: The Wisdom of Property and the Culture of the Middle Classes

1 J. M. Keynes, *The General Theory of Employment, Interest and Money* (London: Macmillan & Co.1936): Chapter 12.

2 An implication of the recent zero net saving in the household sectors of the United States and Great Britain is that households forced by debt to consume less than their incomes have their counterpart in households that consume in excess of their incomes.

Chapter 14: The Limitations of Financial Stabilisation by Central Banks

1 M. Kalecki, 'Multilateralism and Full Employment' in J. Osiatyński (ed.) *The Collected Works of Michał Kalecki, Volume I Capitalism: Business Cycles and Full Employment* (Oxford: The Clarendon Press 1990).

2 V. Chick, 'The Evolution of the Banking System and the Theory of Saving, Investment and Interest' in V. Chick *On Money, Method and Keynes,*

Selected Essays edited by Philip Arestis and Sheila C. Dow (London: Macmillan 1992).

3 J. Toporowski, *The End of Finance: The Theory of Capital Market Inflation, Financial Derivatives and Pension Fund Capitalism* (London: Routledge 2000).

4 R. G. Hawtrey, *Currency and Credit* (London: Longmans, Green and Co. 1927): chapter XIV. Unfortunately for believers in gold convertibility, its resumption in 1925 was associated with deflation and a further decline in international trade.

5 See J. Halevi, 'The Argentine Crisis' *Monthly Review* Vol. 53, No. 11, March 2002; N. Levy-Orlik, 'The Effect of Open Market Operations in Emerging Markets' Paper presented to the Union for Radical Political Economy at the American Social Sciences Association Meetings in Washington, DC on the 5 January 2003.

6 J. Halevi, 'The Argentine Crisis', op. cit.

7 An exception is R. S. Sayers, 'Central Banking in Underdeveloped Countries' in *Central Banking after Bagehot* (Oxford: The Clarendon Press 1957).

Index

Index

Index

Index

Lightning Source UK Ltd.
Milton Keynes UK
UKOW050044201211

184069UK00001B/6/P